Hadrian

James Morwood

BLOOMSBURY

LONDON • NEW DELHI • NEW YORK • SYDNEY

Bloomsbury Academic

An imprint of Bloomsbury Publishing Plc

50 Bedford Square
London
WC1B 3DP
UK

1385 Broadway
New York
NY 10018
USA

www.bloomsbury.com

Bloomsbury is a registered trade mark of Bloomsbury Publishing Plc

First published 2013

British Library Cataloguing-in-Publication Data
A catalogue record for this book is available from the British Library.

ISBN: PB: 978-1-8496-6886-6
ePub: 978-1-7809-3477-8
ePDF: 978-1-7809-3476-1

Library of Congress Cataloging-in-Publications Data
A catalog record for this book is available from the Library of Congress.

Typeset by Fakenham Prepress Solutions, Fakenham, Norfolk NR21 8NN
Printed and bound in Great Britain

Contents

List of Figures

List of Figures

Introduction

This is the shilling life.[1] Anthony R. Birley, a leading scholar of the period, published the 400-odd tightly packed pages of his masterly *Hadrian, The Restless Emperor* in 1997. A particularly impressive feature of his shrewdly insightful book is that he is able to suggest where and in whose company Hadrian may have been at any given stage of his career. A dazzling array of illustrations as well as a fine extended essay on our subject are on offer in Thorsten Opper's catalogue to the Hadrian exhibition which he mounted in the British Museum in 2008. Among many valuable aspects of this latter publication is the light it casts on the current archaeological state of play. Any modern book on Hadrian will inevitably be greatly in debt to Birley and Opper, and I am delighted to acknowledge how much I owe them. A further entrant to the lists is Anthony Everett, who in 2009 published *Hadrian and the Triumph of Rome*, again a book of some 400 pages which usefully establishes the context for the emperor's career. It is a somewhat old-fashioned, gracefully written biography – and none the worse for that.

However, the figure of Hadrian is particularly well suited to the shorter compass of this *Ancients in Action* series. Like the 'shilling life' of W. H. Auden's poem 'Who's Who', it will give you all the facts, including how 'Love made him weep his pints like you and me'. So much of what we think we know about Hadrian is in fact uncertain. Admittedly, we have a considerable number of relevant contemporary inscriptions and some illuminating documents on papyrus from Egypt. Unfortunately, however, we possess only two literary sources for Hadrian's life, both dating from much later. The first is Book 69 of Dio Cassius' *Roman History*, a survey

which led from Romulus to the early decades of the third century
AD when Dio was writing. A senator from Bithynia (north-west
Turkey), and possibly reflecting a senatorial bias against Hadrian,
he was, according to Dominic Rathbone, 'a diligent and intelligent
compiler, whose account of the imperial period is sharpened and
coloured by his personal experiences of government under the
emperors of varying quality from Commodus to Severus Alexander
(176–235)'.[2] It is thus highly regrettable that Book 69, like most
of the *History*, survives only in excerpts and epitomes, the latter
mainly made by the eleventh-century Byzantine monk Xiphilinus.
Thus there are vast omissions and abrupt transitions in the text
that has survived.

The second literary source is even more flawed. This is the
biography of Hadrian, purportedly by Aelius Spartianus, in the
Historia Augusta, a set of lives for all the emperors from Hadrian
to Carinus (117–284). These lives were written towards the end of
the fourth century, though for some unknown reason the author
claimed to be six different people writing between 284 and 337.
While most of the later and minor biographies are – the words are
Rathbone's – 'confections of fantasy iced with fake documents', the
earlier ones, including Hadrian's, carry decidedly more conviction
and were probably based on the lives of the emperors written by
Marius Maximus, a contemporary of Dio. Even so, a question mark
must hang over everything they say.

In view of the problems arising from the nature of the sources, it is
hardly surprising that Birley frankly admits that in his account 'there
have to be (all too often, perhaps) turns of phrase such as "probably",
"plausibly enough", "it may be conjectured"'.[3] The narrower format
of my book precludes me from entering into too many such areas
of uncertainty, though it is neither possible nor desirable to avoid
them altogether. I have attempted – and no doubt failed – to
eschew imaginative reconstruction such as we find in Marguerite

Yourcenar's once-famous *Memoirs of Hadrian* (1951), and to emulate the approach that Thomas Hobbes (rather optimistically) identified in Thucydides, that he does not 'enter into men's hearts, further than the Actions themselves evidently guide him'. Of course, in Hadrian's case, as we have seen, many, if not most, of 'the Actions' are decidedly labile. At all events, I trust that I have said enough to allow readers to make up their minds as to the validity of Edward Gibbon's judgement in *The Decline and Fall of the Roman Empire* (1776) in so far as it applies to Hadrian:

> If a man were called to fix the period in the history of the world, during which the condition of the human race was most happy and prosperous, he would, without hesitation, name that which elapsed from the death of Domitian to the accession of Commodus. The vast extent of the Roman empire was governed by absolute power, under the guidance of virtue and wisdom. The armies were restrained by the firm but gentle hand of four successive emperors, whose characters and authority commanded involuntary respect. The forms of civil administration were carefully preserved by Nerva, Trajan, Hadrian, and the Antonines, who delighted in the image of liberty, and were pleased with considering themselves as the accountable ministers of the laws.

At the same time, I also hope that over the course of these pages an impression will emerge of a remarkable man whose character has many, at times contradictory facets.

I would like to express my warm gratitude to Stephen Anderson, Keith Maclennan (not least for his Cumbrian expertise on Hadrian's Wall), Christopher Mallan, Peter Thonemann, Mathieu de Bakker and the admirable readers for Bloomsbury Academic for their most helpful comments on my drafts. Thanks are also due to Deborah Blake and Charlotte Loveridge of Duckworth and Bloomsbury respectively for their constant encouragement and support, to Sarah Gray for typing out the pencilled manuscript, and to Dominic West of Fakenham Prepress Solutions for his ever-courteous efficiency. I am grateful to Martin Hammond and E. J. Kenney for allowing me to print their translations of Thucydides and Apuleius respectively.

James Morwood
Wadham College, Oxford

Note

Abbreviations of names, texts, etc. are explained in the first section (*Classical Works*) of the Bibliography.

Chronology

AD

	11 August: Hadrian proclaimed emperor
118	9 July: Hadrian enters Rome as emperor
121	21 April: Foundation ceremony for Temple of Venus and Rome
121–125	Hadrian starts on first journey (Gaul, Upper Germany, Raetia, Noricum, Lower Germany, Britain, Spain, Syria, Cappadocia, Bithynia, Asia, Greece, Sicily)
122?	Plotina, Trajan's widow, dies and is deified
128	Hadrian assumes title *Pater Patriae* (Father of the Fatherland)
128–132	Hadrian starts on second journey (Africa, Greece, Asia, Syria, Arabia, Judaea, Egypt, Syria, Thrace, Moesia, Greece)
130	24 October: Antinous drowns in the Nile
	30 October: Antinoopolis founded
122–125/6	Jewish revolt
134	Hadrian in Rome
	Hadrian adopts Lucius Ceionius Commodus
137?	Sabina dies and is deified
138	Lucius Ceionius Commodus dies the night before 1 January
	25 January: Hadrian adopts Titus Aurelius Fulvius Boionius Arrius Antoninus (the future Antoninus Pius); Antoninus adopts Marcus Annius Verus (the future Marcus Aurelius) and the younger Lucius Ceionius Commodus (the future Lucius Verus)
	10 July: Hadrian dies at Baiae

Figure 1 Map of the Roman Empire in 117 AD

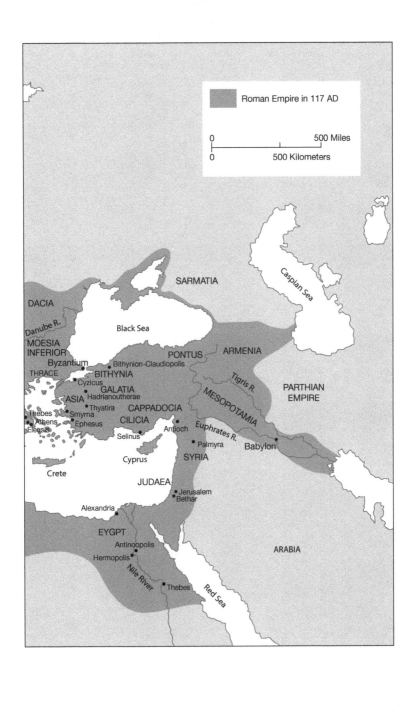

Roman Empire in 117 AD

0   500 Miles

0   500 Kilometers

SARMATIA

Caspian Sea

DACIA

Danube R.

Black Sea

MOESIA
INFERIOR

PONTUS

ARMENIA

Byzantium

Bithynion-Claudiopolis

THRACE

BITHYNIA

Tigris R.

PARTHIAN
EMPIRE

Cyzicus

GALATIA

MESOPOTAMIA

ASIA

Hadrianoutherae

Thyatira

CAPPADOCIA

Thebes

Smyrna

CILICIA

Athens

Ephesus

Euphrates R.

Eleusis

Selinus

Antioch

Babylon

Palmyra

Cyprus

SYRIA

Crete

JUDAEA

Jerusalem

Bethar

Alexandria

ARABIA

EYGPT

Antinoopolis

Hermopolis

Nile River

Thebes

Red Sea

1

Death on the Nile

A central, some modern commentators would say *the* central occurrence in the emperor Hadrian's life came when his youthful lover, the Bithynian Greek Antinous, drowned in the Nile in October 130 AD. This tragic event offers a summation of a number of the features of Hadrian's character that will emerge as fundamental in the course of this study. And since we are dealing with an emperor, it is scarcely surprising that the public and private aspects of his *persona* will prove to be inextricably linked.

Figure 2   Antinous (Altes Museum, Berlin)

After indulging, together with his youthful friend, in his Greek-style passion for hunting in a lion hunt near Alexandria – later to be celebrated in grandiloquent poetry – Hadrian's insatiable wanderlust and his thirst for discovery took him up the Nile through the heart of Egypt. When Antinous drowned, the entirely characteristic reaction of one of the word's great builders was to found a city in his name and to follow this up by establishing an international cult of the young man.

Disconcerting light was soon shone on what was likely to have been the bleak hollowness of his marriage when in mid-November his wife Sabina went off with some of her friends, including her possible lover Balbilla, to visit a famous statue near Egyptian Thebes. Balbilla blithely graffitied the statue with a poem which contains nary a mention of the drowned boy.

While Antinous' feelings towards his imperial lover remain unknown, Hadrian was totally besotted with him. His personal involvement, however, reflects the ideal of Greek love, the passion of an older man for a younger which worked to their mutual benefit. Thus the love affair with Antinous clearly relates at one level to Hadrian's devotion to all things Greek. The young Hadrian had been nicknamed *Graeculus* (little Greek) by his fellows, and as an adult he gave a major boost to the current revival of Greek culture. This culminated in his launch of a vast international Greek Institute, the Panhellenion. Did he appear at the inauguration of its central building with his young Greek boyfriend by his side? We cannot know, but it would certainly have been appropriate.

At the same time, the death of Antinous will lead us to an exploration of possible flaws in Hadrian's character. However understandable his intense sorrow may have been, his emotional breakdown was not regarded as befitting a Roman emperor. In addition, sinister rumours went the rounds. Dio Cassius reports that Antinous may have been offered as a sacrifice:

For Hadrian was … very keen on the curious arts, and made use of divinations and incantations of all kinds. Thus Hadrian honoured Antinous – either on account of his love for him, or because he had gone to his death voluntarily, for a life to be surrendered willingly to achieve what Hadrian intended …[1]

The fact that the emperor asserted in his autobiography that the death was simply an accident scarcely constitutes conclusive evidence of his innocence in the matter.

The ancient sources lay stress on the contradictions in Hadrian's character. And certainly the death of Antinous can serve as a focus on his complexity. The great builder and traveller with his noble passion for knowledge, the dignified emperor who was the supreme advocate of the Greek enlightenment, was at the same time an enthusiastic investigator of black magic, emotionally uncontrolled and, it appears, an abject failure as a husband. Further contradictions will emerge. The picture is indeed kaleidoscopic; and even if we may conclude by sharing Hamlet's view on the impossibility of plucking out the heart of a man's mystery, I hope that this attempt to do so in the case of Hadrian may at least prove interesting and illuminating.

Growing up in Rome and Spain

Though the future emperor Publius Aelius Hadrianus was born, on 24 January 76 AD, probably in Rome, his family background was largely Spanish. His father Aelius Hadrianus Afer came from Italica on the river Baetis (the modern Guadalquivir) and his mother Domitia Paulina from the harbour town of Gades (Cadiz). Hadrianus Afer was a senator – and thus a man with a fortune of more than a million sesterces – and as such was expected to reside in Rome, the imperial capital. Thus it was there that Hadrian spent his youthful years, with his parents, his older sister and his wet-nurse Germana, who was to outlive him. However, it makes good sense to begin a life of this, the most widely travelled of the emperors, away from Rome, in Baetica, the Spanish province from which his family hailed.

The Baetican city of Italica was some eight kilometres up the river Baetis from Hispalis (Seville). It was the family home of the Ulpii and the Trahii or Traii, the ancestors of Trajan, Hadrian's predecessor as emperor and his soon-to-be adoptive father. Men from the provinces had long since been making their mark in Rome, a process hastened at a pivotal moment in 48 AD when the emperor Claudius persuaded the senate that Gauls from across the Alps should be given the right to become magistrates and consequently senators at Rome.[1] Among the Spaniards who had made it to the top was Annaeus Seneca, the emperor Nero's tutor and adviser, who came from Corduba, also on the Baetis but further upstream. A famous – and famously wealthy – Stoic philosopher, Seneca wrote a succession of plays which mediate between Greek and Renaissance drama. He was a cultural figure of immense importance. Then, in 73 and 74 AD, the emperor Vespasian and his son Titus, while serving as censors, went so far as to bestow patrician status on some provincials, including the family of Trajan. It is possible that, by the end of the first century AD, men of Spanish origin constituted nearly a quarter of the Roman senate, a significant marker of social distinction. And a barrier was broken down with far wider social implications when Vespasian at the same time granted Latin status (more than foreign but less than Roman rights) to all Spanish communities that were not yet Roman or Latin. More than half a century before, the geographer Strabo had written of the process of assimilation that 'those who live around the Baetis have completely converted to the Roman way of life, not even remembering their own language any more'.[2]

Baetica was a region of legendary agricultural wealth. Strabo informs us that 'the land through which the Baetis flows is superior in comparison with the whole inhabited world in respect of fertility and the good things that come from the land and the sea'.[3] He tells us, in a no-doubt hyperbolic illustration of their prosperity, that when the Carthaginians attacked the area, they found the inhabitants using silver amphoras for themselves and silver feeding-troughs for their animals.[4] And he writes that no gold, silver, copper or iron of such quality had been found anywhere else.[5] Exports included vast quantities of grain and wine as well as *garum*, a fish sauce that was indispensable in Roman cooking. Consisting of the liquid strained from fish offal saturated in salt and left to ferment, and referred to by Mary Beard as 'that characteristically Roman concoction of decomposing marine life',[6] it was used by the Romans much as we use salt. Surprisingly enough, according to Pliny the Elder it added an appetizing taste to the food.[7] Indeed it was similar to the fermented fish sauces which are a feature of South-East Asian cooking, for example Vietnamese *nuoc-nam*.

Perhaps above all the region was famous for its production of olive oil, and Hadrian's family possessed fertile olive plantations, possibly upstream from Italica. A gold coin issued in Hadrian's reign shows the personified figure of Hispania (Spain) reclining with an olive branch in her right hand. Olive oil was a commodity without which Roman life could scarcely function. It was a key and highly beneficial ingredient in their cooking, just as it is in Mediterranean countries today. It was also used instead of soap and provided the fuel for oil lamps. It was not just for Roman civilians that olive oil was vital. It has been estimated that every one of the army's legions needed 1,370 amphoras of it each year.[8] Thus the oil trade was highly lucrative, and money must have poured into the family coffers.

The scale of the wealth that this trade generated can be illustrated by what happened to the pots that contained the olive oil when they arrived at Rome's harbour on the Tiber. After the oil had been decanted, possibly into bulk containers, in one of the warehouses, the pots had to be broken up. Rancid oil residue in the porous clay meant that they could not be reused. Behind the warehouses there was a triangular hill consisting entirely of broken bits of pottery. Nowadays called Monte Testaccio (Broken Pot Mountain) and crowning one of Rome's best night-life districts, it has a perimeter of more than one kilometre at its base and is variously estimated as 35 and 40 metres high: it is likely that once it was even higher. Dump the hill may have been, but it was an organized one. The pots were carried up the mound, probably four at a time, by donkeys or mules and smashed on level terraces with retaining walls. The broken pottery was stabilized with fragments of lighter pots from Africa and then everything was covered with powdered lime to suppress the reek of rancid oil. Monte Testaccio is a remarkable survivor from ancient Rome, and scrambling up its slippery slopes, now largely – and fortunately – covered with grass, is a stimulating activity. Quite apart from enjoying the splendid view at the top, one feels a sense of awe as one treads on the fragments of at least 24 million amphoras, representing getting on for two thousand million kilograms of olive oil, that lie buried beneath one's feet. As Amanda Claridge remarks, the hill 'symbolizes the "consumer city", swallowing the produce of its mighty empire in a one-way trade, throwing away the "empties" in a heap to one side'.[9] We can well imagine the fabulous wealth of the oil-producing family into which Hadrian was born.

Hadrian's father died in 85 or 86 AD when he was nine, and two guardians were appointed for him, both from Italica. One of them was a knight called P. Acilius Attianus; the other was Hadrian's first cousin once removed, the future emperor Trajan. In 87 or 88, the boy would have begun his secondary education, possibly with the celebrated teacher Q. Terentius Scaurus – the finest grammarian of the age according to Aulus Gellius – as his *grammaticus* (grammar and literature instructor).[10] Hadrian developed a taste for the older authors, the old-school Ennius rather than Virgil among the poets, and the severe Elder Cato and Coelius Antipater, a historian of the Second Punic War, among the prose authors.[11] He also regarded Greek literature more highly than Latin. In this preference, he was in harmony with a vibrant cultural movement of the period from about 60 to 230 AD, dubbed 'the Second Sophistic' by an Athenian writer of the third century. Following in the footsteps of the itinerant sophists (professors of higher education) of the fifth and fourth century BC, its exponents saw Greek declamation as the most prestigious literary activity. Greek culture thus attained an aura of intellectual glamour, and Hadrian eagerly succumbed to its allure.[12] The *Historia Augusta* (from now on *HA*) tells us that he 'was so attracted in this direction that a few people used to call him *Graeculus* (little Greek)', as we have already noted.[13] His passion for all things Greek was to have momentous consequences.

Some time after his fourteenth birthday, Hadrian went to Italica. It has been suggested that he had assumed the *toga virilis* (the man's toga) and thus found himself under some obligation to inspect the family property in Spain. Fourteen would have been an early, though not unprecedented, age for this rite of passage from boyhood to youth.[14] A boy's father or guardian made the decision about the stage when it should take place; but Hadrian's fourteen sounds remarkably precocious in view of the fact that the boy who had undergone it was regarded as sexually mature,[15] and the age of puberty for males may have been far later in the ancient world: under the heading 'The Great Puberty Shift', James Davidson puts it at roughly 18.5 years, against 14.5 today.[16] Davidson's estimate, however, has been seriously challenged; and indeed the Aristotelian *History of Animals* gives it as fourteen.[17] Be that as it may, the ceremony had usually occurred by a young man's seventeenth birthday, the age at which he could enlist in the army.

Whenever Hadrian may have started on his transition to adulthood, it is helpful to look at this first stage of the process and see how it locates the young Roman at a crucial turning point. The ceremony usually took place on 17 March at the festival of Liber, the Roman god of fertility. The boy laid aside the *toga praetexta* with its purple stripe and the amulet of childhood (the *bulla*) in front of the household gods and, after putting on the *toga virilis* worn by all adult males, proceeded to the Forum of Augustus where the ceremony of transition occurred. Here stood the temple of Mars the Avenger, vowed by the young Augustus after the battle of Philippi in celebration of the revenge that he had taken on Brutus and Cassius, the assassins of his adoptive father Julius Caesar. At the centre of the forum stood Augustus' statue as Father of his country, and all around were images of famous Roman statesmen and generals from the heroic past. It was here that the boy became a Roman citizen. For Hadrian, as for all other young Romans, the setting laid unmistakable stress on filial duty, on service to the state and, especially as war was traditionally resolved upon in the temple of Mars, on military obligation. This was the day on which the boy emerged as an individual, now using his *praenomen*, his first name, Publius in Hadrian's case. It concluded in celebratory vein with feasting and the festival of Liber, the Italian god of fertility.[18]

The male journey into adulthood did not end here, however. The boy had become a *iuvenis* (youth), not a man. Roman girls left their childhood behind on the eve of their marriage in their late teens or early twenties (elite marriages often took place earlier). They would dedicate their toys and dolls to the household gods and, it was thought, emerge as adults over the course of the next day. Male youths, on the other hand, were seen as prone to – and easily led into – violence, aggression and lack of sexual self-control. Clearly the macho qualities at times only too visible in the young Roman male were in their way healthy markers in a society whose mythology told that Mars, the sexually intemperate god of warfare, was the father of Romulus, the founder of Rome, who with his brother Remus was suckled by a wolf. However, these qualities needed to be harnessed and disciplined for the public good, and an upper-class youth would receive guidance by associating with an older man who would mould his character to Roman ideals. Cicero describes his own youthful experience as follows:

> When I had formally put on the *toga virilis* I was taken by my father
> to the lawyer Quintus Mucius Scaevola. The idea was that – as far
> as was humanly possible – I should never leave the old man's sight.
> There were all manner of things that Scaevola used to talk about with
> intelligence and penetration. I formed the habit of memorizing all his
> epigrammatic remarks as a useful addition to my knowledge.[19]

It should perhaps be added that a sexual element would have been entirely inappropriate in a relationship such as the one Cicero describes.

The cutting of the first beard, celebrated with a sacrifice of bullocks and the dedication of the cut beard to a deity, was viewed as the end of a period of undisciplined behaviour and a step closer to adulthood. The hope was that, by his marriage in his mid twenties, the Roman male had completed the transition to adulthood and was ripe for involvement in politics. Hadrian both got married and entered the senate at the age of 24.

Figure 3   The young Hadrian (Minneapolis Institute of Arts)

Whether or not he had assumed the *toga virilis* when he went to Spain, it appears that, after his arrival, the youthful Hadrian joined the *iuvenes* (the young men), the local organization for youths from top families.[20] Next to nothing is known about their activities, but they presumably engaged in physical and probably in quasi-military activity. These groups of young blades could have a bad reputation, very much in line with the dangers inherent in the youthful temperament discussed above. In Apuleius' novel *The Golden Ass*, a young beauty warns her lover to go home early because 'there is a gang of young men of good family disturbing the public peace just now. You can see murdered men lying in the open street.'[21] And other evidence suggests that such behaviour was not restricted to fiction.[22] However, perhaps disappointingly, there is nothing to suggest that Hadrian and his fellows got up to anything untoward. What the *HA* does tell us is that he was 'so fond of hunting that he incurred criticism for it, and for this reason Trajan recalled him from his homeland.'[23] If this is true, the older man was certainly doing his job in keeping an eye on the youngster and watching out for foibles. For the Greeks, hunting was a noble pursuit and a feature of their heroic literature. Xenophon, the Athenian soldier and writer of the fifth and fourth centuries BC, had extolled its benefits in a monograph with the enthusiasm of an aficionado: 'it makes those who practise it healthy of body and better at seeing and hearing, it keeps them young for longer, and it gives them the best training for war.'[24] (The Bithynian Arrian, who later became Hadrian's friend, was to update Xenophon's book in the light of the revolution in the sport brought about by the Celtic greyhound. He named his own dogs after Xenophon's.)[25] However, it was not yet deemed appropriate for upper-class Romans. Ovid's splendidly epic account of the hunt of the Calydonian boar in his *Metamorphoses* is subverted by a sly touch of humour when the aged hero Nestor, eager to escape the quarry's onrush, uses his spear to pole-vault to the safety of a tree.[26] Thus Hadrian's love of hunting was a symptom of the *Graeculus* identity. Writing of Hadrian when emperor and his youthful boyfriend Antinous, Caroline Vout draws attention to some surviving papyrus fragments and a four-line chunk of poetry which commemorate what is taken to be a lion hunt in Libya in which they were the leading participants. 'But,' she remarks of the pieces of written evidence, 'they sound too many warning bells to be interpreted as evidence for a real hunt' since the hunt supplies a metaphor for eroticism or amorous pursuit.[27] However, it is surely allowable to view the hunt *both* literally *and* metaphorically. We may be forgiven for feeling that Hadrian in love could also be Hadrian the hunting enthusiast.

What did Hadrian feel about Italica after his stay there? Always a healthy trencherman, he may have been grateful if it was here that he was introduced to what we are told became his favourite dish, a game pie consisting of sow's udder, pheasant and ham baked in pastry.[28] The fact that he never went to Italica when he was in Spain as emperor may suggest that he took against the place. On the other hand, he was extraordinarily generous to it, proving the driving force behind a walled extension of the town comprising a temple, baths, an amphitheatre and other public buildings.[29] The amphitheatre was one of the largest in the whole empire. Thus the message we receive about Hadrian's attitude to Italica is a mixed one. Sadly, his new town was not destined to last long. The hill upon which it was set consisted of extremely unstable clay. It is indeed surprising that it was possible to build it in the first place, and, within little more than a century, many of its great houses had been abandoned. According to travellers, wheat was being grown in the amphitheatre in the eighteenth century. But, before Hadrian's additions suffered this Ozymandias-like fate, Italica's new grandeur caused it to eclipse Hispalis down the river in importance.

Trajan was also in Spain at the time of Hadrian's visit, in command of the country's sole legion, VII Gemina, but returned to Rome to take up the consulship at the start of 91. Hadrian, who, we are told, was regarded by Trajan 'as a son', went back to Rome too, no doubt as a result of his guardian's summons.[30] His career was about to begin, and the Roman world lay all before him.

The Greek connection

HA 3.1 tells us that in 101, Hadrian read a speech by the Emperor Trajan to the senate and 'provoked laughter with his somewhat rustic accent'. The account goes on to tell us that he 'then worked hard on his Latin until he became highly proficient and fluent'. The fact that Hadrian was brought up in Rome makes this hard to believe, and the suggestion that the time he had spent in the army by then had debased his pronunciation is hard to swallow. A magisterial new German edition of the *Historia* asserts, reasonably enough, that the whole incident must be a fiction.[31] Even so, a report of his mocking reception raises the question of how the influx of Spaniards and their ever-increasing influence which we outlined at the start of the chapter was viewed by the Roman elite.

In a satirical portrait of a racist he calls Umbricius, the poet Juvenal, Hadrian's contemporary, directs his scorn not at Spaniards but at Greeks, and there is little evidence of anti-Spanish feeling at Rome. In any case, James Uden has remarked on the destabilizing irony of the fact that Juvenal's Umbricius is fleeing the Greeks of Rome in order to settle in the ultra-Greek city of Cumae in southern Italy.[32] Yet his racist attack on the Greeks has its own relevance to Hadrian and his passion for all that was Greek, a passion not necessarily in harmony with the standard Roman view of things. Umbricius fulminates:

> I shan't hesitate to tell you what nation is most popular with our wealthy men and which people I take special care to avoid, and I won't be ashamed to do so. My fellow Romans, I can't tolerate a Greek Rome! But in fact how small a portion of these dregs are from the Greek mainland! For ages now the Syrian river Orontes has flowed into the Tiber … The Greeks are quick-witted, shamelessly bold, glib in their talk which pours forth more torrentially than Isaeus' rhetoric. Say what you think he is. He has brought himself among us to transform himself into anything you want him to be: grammar teacher, rhetorician, geometrician, painter, masseur, augurer, tightrope walker, doctor, magician – your starving little Greek (*Graeculus*) knows how to be all of these. [33]

In the final line, Hadrian's nickname *Graeculus* reverberates with scathing contempt. It is important, of course, not to take satirical hyperbole literally, but there is no doubt that at some level Umbricius' diatribe reflects, even if through a distorting magnifying glass, the at best ambivalent attitude of Romans towards Greeks.

Starting Out

For the senatorial order Rome under Domitian, the current emperor, was not necessarily a very safe place to be. He was becoming increasingly tyrannical, and those who seemed to oppose him were eliminated. The historian Tacitus, whose political career blossomed under Domitian, wondered to what avail the opponents had martyred themselves.[1] Compliant he may have been, but even so his portrayal of Domitian in his biography of his father-in-law, the general Agricola, is a devastating exposé of darkly malevolent hypocrisy: the emperor's red complexion furnished him with a mask against shame.[2] Yet the poet Martial sang his praises with unrestrained rapture, identifying that very redness with a sense of shame and basic decency.[3] Hadrian's patron Trajan was completely loyal to him, moving swiftly to Upper Germany in 89 AD to deal with a would-be usurper.

Back in Rome, Hadrian embarked on a political career. At the age of eighteen, he became a member of a board of ten which adjudicated lawsuits.[4] From this not undemanding but low-key initiation into public life, he moved on to a prestigious position standing in for consuls when they were away at a festival outside Rome. Then he became one of six squadron leaders in the annual parade of the Roman *equites* (knights, the social rank below senators) on 15 July.[5] He was very clearly getting the right kind of exposure.

He now joined the army as the military tribune of Legion II Adiutrix at Aquincum (Budapest) on the Danube.[6] The cadre of the higher officers was still largely recruited from young members of the families of senators or equites who gained their training through practical military activity. Even so, it is somewhat startling that this novice was now, in theory at least, second-in-command of an experienced unit in an important frontier province. In 96 AD, he transferred to Legion V Macedonica in Lower Moesia, also on the Danube.[7]

On 18 September of that year, Domitian was assassinated in a palace plot, and the senate replaced him with the 65-year-old and childless Marcus Cocceius Nerva. With his circle of aged advisers, Nerva had no solid power base. Some thirteen months later, in October 97 AD, the Praetorian Guard mutinied and forced the new emperor, who was vomiting in his panic, to hand over Domitian's killers. They were summarily lynched by the troops. Nerva desperately needed the support of the army and a strong family network. His inspired solution was to adopt Trajan, who would supply him with both.[8]

Hadrian was sent to Trajan, now serving on the Rhine, to congratulate him on behalf of the legions in Lower Moesia.[9] When Trajan moved from Upper to Lower Germany, he ensured that people close to him were in positions of authority in the former region: Hadrian was appointed military tribune of Legion XXII Primigenia and his brother-in-law, Julius Servianus, an associate of Trajan's, took over the command. The relationship between Hadrian and Servianus was always to prove tense. According to the *HA*, the latter reported to Trajan that Hadrian was spending money extravagantly and getting into debt.[10]

Nerva died on 27 January 98 AD, and the next day, Trajan was declared emperor. Hadrian and his brother-in-law were both eager to be the first to inform him.[11] The *HA* tells us that Servianus sent his own messenger and sabotaged Hadrian's carriage, but even so, Hadrian reached the new emperor before Servianus' man. Whether true or false, the story is symptomatic of the corrosive rivalry mentioned in the last paragraph that was to last until Servianus' death soon before Hadrian's own.

Keeping Hadrian with him, Trajan took measures to secure stability in Germany and the Danube provinces. He eventually arrived in Rome late in 99 AD. The *HA* records that Hadrian now became a favourite of Trajan's, but tensions developed as a result of the complaints about Hadrian's behaviour with certain 'boys whom Trajan loved immoderately' from their guardians.[12] It looks as if Hadrian was muscling in too aggressively on the emperor's amorous territory. We shall discuss later the same-sex relationships that were a feature of both Trajan's and Hadrian's courts. It may be worth remarking here that, in these soldier-emperors' armies, men who engaged in homosexual acts (presumably sodomy) were clubbed to death, a process called *fustuarium*.[13] Different standards were clearly applied beneath the high command.

Any tensions between Trajan and Hadrian were short-lived, and in 100 AD, their relationship was cemented by a marriage between Hadrian and Trajan's great niece Sabina.[14] The groom was 24, his bride probably 15. It is unlikely that love played any part in the match. Indeed, the *HA* records the remark of one commentator, that it was 'very little desired by Hadrian himself'.[15] His devotion in fact went to

Figure 4   Trajan

his mother-in-law Matidia, a particular favourite of Trajan's who had urged the marriage. The main significance of the union was that it marked out Hadrian as a possible heir to the childless emperor.

Hadrian now embarked upon a career in the senate, possibly also serving as a priest of the deified emperor Augustus.[16] But then, in March 101, he went with Trajan as a *comes* (a companion of the emperor, an aide-de-camp) to Dacia (roughly speaking, today's Romania and Moldova) to deal with the Dacian king Decebalus. Here, the *HA* informs us, he indulged in wine, 'so as to fall in with Trajan's habits' and was very richly rewarded for this by the emperor.[17] He may well not have remained there for the two years of the successful campaign, but have returned to Rome to hold the post of tribune of the people for the year 102 AD.[18] Two years later he was elected praetor for 105.[19] Trajan stumped up a considerable sum of money to pay for the games he had to stage in this office. In fact, they were held in Hadrian's absence. Decebalus was causing trouble again[20] and war was declared on Dacia in May 105. Trajan set out for the area, taking Hadrian with him as commander of Legion I Minervia.[21] The army, consisting of about 120,000 men, was the largest single expedition ever mounted by the Romans.[22]

Hadrian served in Dacia for most of the campaign, which ended with the capture of the Dacian capital and King Decebalus' suicide. The *HA* tells us that Hadrian's many outstanding deeds became renowned;[23] and Trajan awarded him military decorations, as he had in the first campaign.[24] When Trajan gave him a diamond ring which he had been given by Nerva, Hadrian saw this as another sign that he was the emperor's choice of successor.[25]

We have a stunning pictorial record of the Dacian Wars on Trajan's column in Rome, which was erected in 113 to celebrate the emperor's successes.[26] The column was topped with a statue of Trajan, and his remains were later entombed in its base. Carvings, which may have been added in Hadrian's reign,[27] spiral around this sensational monument, celebrating not only the valour of the Roman army but also its remarkable technical achievements. We see the Romans' new stone bridge over the Danube built by Trajan's architect, Apollodorus of Damascus – with whom Hadrian was later to clash, though how seriously remains uncertain (see Chapter 6) – as well as the more mundane building of defences, camps, forts, bridges and roads by the Roman legionaries. The celebration of the army's technical achievements is reflected in an inscription of a speech which Hadrian was to give when emperor to his troops in Africa, praising them in some detail for building a lengthy wall – a task that others would have spread over several days – in just one.[28] Dio Cassius pays tribute to Hadrian's interest not merely in the usual appurtenances of camps, such as weapons, engines, trenches, ramparts and palisades, but also in the private affairs of each individual, both of the men serving in the ranks and of the officers – though part of his motivation was his wish to cut back on luxurious military lifestyles![29]

Figure 5 A field dressing station portrayed on Trajan's column. On the right a dresser, holding a roll of bandage, attends, an auxiliary soldier with a wound in his thigh. In his pain the soldier grits his teeth and clutches the rock he is sitting on. In the centre a medical officer examines a legionary soldier. © Science Museum/Science & Society Picture Library

Hadrian and the soldiers

Writing probably in the early third century AD, Dio Cassius gives a vivid impression of Hadrian as a leader of men:

> He trained the soldiers for every type of battle and some he honoured while others he admonished; and he taught them all they should do. And in order that they should be benefited by observing his example, he everywhere maintained a rigorous lifestyle, and he always walked or rode on horseback, on no occasion at that time getting onto a chariot or four-horsed vehicle. He didn't cover his head either in hot or cold weather, but both in the snows of Germany and in the scorching heat of Egypt he went about with his head bare. To sum up, both by his practice and his precepts he trained and disciplined his army so effectively over the whole empire that even now the methods that he then instituted are observed by soldiers on campaign.[30]

As well as portraying the courage and accomplishments of the Roman army, the column portrays its brutality, though the Dacians outdo the Romans in this regard. Remarkably, it even includes a scene of Roman cowardice when a legionnaire is shown turning his back to the enemy and retreating without his shield. It graphically illustrates the ups and downs of war: a happy scene showing Trajan granting gifts to his soldiers is juxtaposed with one of the death of naked Roman captives, humiliated and tortured by Dacian women. And, perhaps surprisingly, sympathy with the enemy is on display. The last scene of all shows the native population, the men weighted down with packages as they leave their country in front of and beyond the mountains. As they drive their cattle forward, they look back on the land they have lost, facing the new Roman settlers with unflinching dignity.

Future wars would never prove as profitable for the Romans as the two Dacian campaigns. The booty they captured was equivalent in value to more than 700 tons of silver.[31] This paid for both wars and still left a great deal over. Dacia became a province of the Empire, its rich gold mines bringing in still more profit. But, as we shall see, Trajan did not know where to stop.

4

War and Peace

Hadrian did not participate in the triumphant conclusion of the Dacian war. That was pre-empted by his appointment as governor of the province of Lower Pannonia, also on the Danube frontier, where he took command of Legion II Adiutrix, the very legion with which he had begun his military career.[1] Here, from the governor's palace on an island in the Danube,[2] he played a key role by guarding the Romans' western flank. Then, in 108 AD, at the age of 32, he became consul – we do not know whether he served *in absentia* or returned to Rome – and, according to the *HA*, he was told that Trajan planned to adopt him, 'and he was no longer despised and ignored by Trajan's friends.'[3] Whether or not Trajan *had* decided on this course of action, there is no reason to disbelieve the *HA*'s assertion that he became a speech-writer for the emperor.[4]

Three years later, Hadrian went to Athens, probably visiting the lame Stoic philosopher Epictetos at Nicopolis on the way. The man who bore the nickname *Graeculus* was made truly at home in Athens. He was given Athenian citizenship and became a member of a *deme* (a local citizen unit). Then in 112, he was elected *archon eponymos*, the Athenians' chief magistrate after whom their year was named. A bronze statue of Hadrian was erected amid the grandees' seats at the heart of the theatre of Dionysus. Such proved the auspicious start of a relationship of profound mutual admiration. Hadrian was later to declare, 'You know that I use every excuse to do good both to the city as a whole and to Athenian citizens individually.'[5]

Images of Hadrian as emperor regularly portray him as bearded. While Romans of the old school from the second century BC and before had worn long beards, for some two centuries shaving had been habitual. The earliest emperor Augustus had established the image of the clean-shaven first citizen. Was Hadrian making a statement by overhauling this ideal? Since it was the Greek tradition to wear beards, the *Graeculus* may have been aiming to project a Greek identity. Opper, on the other hand, suggests that the beard was the badge of a military man of the younger generation.[6] And indeed, by the third century, emperors were regularly wearing shaggy beards to show their solidarity with their fellow soldiers, their shared shagginess being later transmogrified into crew-cuts and designer stubble.[7] It may be that both factors underlie Hadrian's decision. After all, he was both a soldier and a man with a deep commitment to all things Greek. But such speculations may in fact be beside the point: the *HA* reports that he grew his beard to cover the natural blemishes on his face.[8]

At this point, in 114, Trajan gathered an army against Parthia, Rome's long-standing and highly problematic enemy. The *casus belli* was that one of its three rival kings, Chosroes, had deposed the king of Armenia and replaced him with his own candidate in violation of the treaty that stipulated that Rome should nominate the Armenian king. Passing through Athens, Trajan made Hadrian a member of his staff and proceeded with him to Syria. Their closeness is indicated by the fact that when Trajan made an offering to local manifestations of Zeus, Hadrian wrote the verse inscription which accompanied it.[9] Dio tells a story of this time, which well illustrates Trajan's susceptibility to youthful male beauty. Abgarus, ruler of a small kingdom on the Euphrates, was hoping to remain neutral by avoiding any straightforward alliance with the Parthians or the Romans. When he realized that he could sit on the fence no longer, he anxiously sought an alliance with Trajan.

Partly persuaded by his son Arbandes who was beautiful and in the prime of his youth and for this reason in favour with Trajan, and partly in fear of the latter's presence, Abgarus then met him on his journey, made an apology and obtained pardon; for he had a splendid intercessor in the boy. As a result of this he became Trajan's friend and entertained him to dinner, and during the dinner he brought on the boy to perform a barbarian dance.[10]

Trajan was delighted by the boy, especially by his gold earrings,[11] and any problems melted away.

From Syria, Trajan moved to Armenia and deposed and executed the new king, declaring the country a Roman province. After a number of victories, he captured Ctesiphon, the ancient Parthian winter capital, in 116. He was hailed as *Parthicus* and three celebratory days of circus games were held in Rome.

Trajan's achievement had indeed been dazzling. Since the shattering defeat the Parthians had inflicted on Crassus in 53 BC, no previous Roman general had fought them with anything like complete success or managed to reach the Parthian capital. In the aftermath of the campaign, Hadrian was appointed governor of Syria, and the empress Plotina, ever his devoted patroness, secured his designation as consul for 118.[12] The victorious Trajan was less fortunate: already ill, he now suffered a stroke and became partly paralysed. In the summer of 117, he resolved to return to Rome, but died on his way there, at Selinus in Cilicia. He adopted Hadrian on his deathbed, though, as the *HA* tells us, there were those who raised doubts over this.[13]

Hadrian's succession as emperor was not a foregone conclusion. According to the *HA*, malicious gossip reported that 'he had corrupted Trajan's freedmen, had cultivated his boy favourites and had often had sexual relations with them at the time when he was an inner member of the court'.[14] However that may be, there was discontent at Rome, and the guard prefect Attianus executed four senators, all of them ex-consuls, whom he suspected of plotting against Hadrian.[15]

(They were killed at or while travelling to their homes outside Rome.) Although Domitian had executed at least twelve former consuls in the previous generation, the senate was appalled and, even when the new emperor at once disassociated himself from Attianus' actions and promised that such an event would never occur again,[16] these brutal killings darkened his relations with that body throughout his reign. Understandably, he made a bid for popularity with the masses by remitting debts to the state treasury, burning the records of these debts in the Forum of Trajan with arresting publicity.[17]

Trajan had died with his image of the great military expansionist, the Alexander of his day as he saw himself, largely intact. But, as the *HA* reports:

> The nations which Trajan had conquered revolted. The Moors were making attacks, the Sarmatians waging war, the Britons could not be contained under Roman control, Egypt was in a ferment of revolt, and finally Libya and Palestine were giving vent to their spirit of rebellion.[18]

Figure 6 Soldiers of the Praetorian Guard carrying containers of wax tablets for burning. © Devonshire Collection, Chatsworth. Reproduced by permission of Chatsworth Settlement Trustees

In the first half of 116 AD, a revolt of the Jewish diaspora had erupted in Cyrenaica (where, according to Dio, 220,000 Greeks and Romans were killed), Egypt and Cyprus (240,000).[19] In what must have struck Hadrian's contemporaries as an astonishing reversal of imperial policy, he decided to evacuate the provinces of Mesopotamia, Assyria and Greater Armenia forthwith. A perilous situation in Dacia led to the abandonment of great swathes of Trajan's conquests in the Danube region.[20] With telling symbolism, the superstructure of Apollodorus' great stone bridge over the Danube was dismantled to stop attacking enemy forces from crossing it.[21] Through an enormously skilful balancing act, Hadrian contrived to celebrate Trajan's achievement and project a military persona for

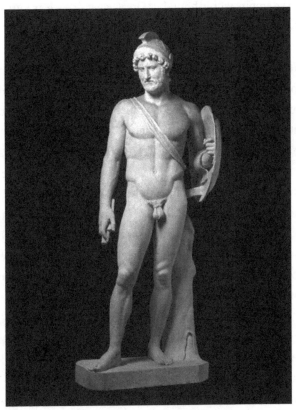

Figure 7   Hadrian as Mars. © Capitoline Museums, Rome

himself – the fine statue of Hadrian as Mars, the god of war, in the
Capitoline Museum at Rome (Figure 7) is a striking example of this
– while undoing large parts of what his predecessor had achieved. To
some – doubtless including the historian Tacitus who planted implied
criticism of Hadrian's policy of quietism in his *Annals*, his history of
the early empire – such retrenchment will have seemed a betrayal of
Rome's greatness.[22] However, as the *HA* rightly observes, Hadrian was
in fact resuming the policy of the early emperors, when he 'devoted his
efforts to maintaining peace throughout the world'.[23] After the disaster
in 9 AD when the Germans had wiped out three Roman legions in the
Teutoburg forest, Augustus had written in his own hand of his 'policy of
keeping the empire within bounds'.[24] Great generals such as Agricola and
Trajan himself, ever emulous of Alexander the Great, inevitably wanted
to push those boundaries ever further. The responsible ruler would view
the matter in a very different light. Virgil, the leading poet of imperial
Rome, had Jupiter declare in his great epic, the *Aeneid*, that he had 'given
the Romans an empire without end',[25] but poetic hyperbole is an entirely
different matter from rational imperial control.

In a straightforwardly literal way, Hadrian certainly set limits to the
Roman empire. In addition to the barriers he constructed in Germany
and Africa, there is his famous wall in the north of Britain, 80 miles
(129 kilometres) long and linking the Tyne estuary to the Solway firth.
Built by legionaries when Hadrian visited Britain in 122 AD, the wall
was a development of existing arrangements. It was punctuated by a
small fort or milecastle every mile. Some of the wall was formed of
turf, but mainly it was built of stone blocks facing a clay and rubble
core. The blocks were covered in whitewash, creating 'a shining white
northern barrier, mirroring the cliffs of Dover to the south', as Sam
Moorhead and David Stuttard neatly observe.[26] For most of its length,
the wall was 10 feet broad, 14 feet high and fronted by a ditch 30 feet
deep containing sharpened wooden branches to the north. It was the
most complex and expensive of all Rome's frontier works.

Figure 8 Hadrian's Wall

The frontier arrangements of Agricola, the father-in-law of the historian Tacitus and Britain's most famous governor (from 77 to 84 AD), had consisted of a series of forts along the valleys of the rivers Tyne, Irthing and Eden. With the wall, Hadrian moved the frontier up to the top of the hills northward of this line; he then moved several of the forts up too and accommodated them within the wall. He also created a militarized buffer zone by constructing, immediately to the south of the wall, a huge and elaborate system of earthworks now known as the *vallum*. Between the wall and the *vallum* ran a military road. The result of all this is an immensely complicated structure of wall, turrets, milecastles, forts, road and *vallum*. Furthermore, the wall crosses two substantial rivers, the North Tyne and the Irthing: there were massive bridges over them of which there are significant remains. Excavation in the forts, especially Housesteads, Chesters and Birdoswald, has revealed extensive detail about the lifestyle of their occupants and about the history of the military units which were stationed there and thanks to their pay brought prosperity to the region. At Vindolanda, one of Agricola's forts nearest to the wall, a very substantial number of preserved documents have been found, the closest approach in any part of the empire to the papyrus treasures of the Egyptian desert.

The *HA* tells us that Hadrian 'often, in very many places in which the barbarians are separated not by rivers but by boundaries, marked the barbarians off with great posts driven deep into the ground like a wall'.[27] This certainly seems to be true of the great palisade he built at the border of Germany for which massive oak posts were split in two and the flat sides fixed outwards by cross-beams.[28] But the wall in Britain and the later fortified line known as the *Fossatum Africae*, built with mud bricks over a length of 60 kilometres at the south of the province of Africa, seem to have been intended not simply as defensive barriers but also with the aims of controlling the native population and expanding the area of Roman influence.[29] There were outposts to the north of Hadrian's Wall and to the south of the *Fossatum Africae*. In addition, the crossing points in the walls were useful for the collection of taxes and other dues. Hadrian's structures were not designed just to keep people out, like Israel's West Bank barrier wall, or to keep people in, like the Berlin Wall. They projected a massive imperial self-confidence.

Romanization – the down side

The biographer and historian Tacitus gives an acid account of the corrosive effect of the Roman way of life on the Britons under the governorship of their country by his father-in-law Agricola between 77 and 84 AD. It would, of course, have been impossible for Agricola to make such radical changes over seven years, but the point about the corrupting influence of Romanization still stands. It is in line with Tacitus' tendency to laud the simplicity of foreign races at the expense of an immoral Roman elite:

> The people were scattered and uncivilized and thus prone to warfare, and in order that they should become accustomed to peace and quiet through a more pleasant lifestyle, he would help communities to build temples, *fora* [city centres] and houses by praising the eager and criticizing the uncommitted. Thus competition to receive his compliments took the place of compulsion. Furthermore, he would train the sons of the chieftains in a liberal education, expressing his preference for the talents of the Britons over the trained abilities of the Gauls. The consequence was that those who had recently refused to speak Latin now wanted to master rhetoric. As a result, even our dress came to be appreciated and the toga was frequently worn. And little by little they departed from the straight and narrow, seduced by the allurements of evil ways: promenades, bath houses and elegant dinner parties. So it came about that the innocent Britons called it all civilization when it was really a factor in their slavery. [30]

Hadrian's wife Sabina had accompanied him to Britain, though it seems unlikely that she had gone with him to the north. Their marriage appears to have been a profoundly unhappy one. Sabina is quoted as saying that, in order to protect the human race, she had ensured she would not conceive a child by Hadrian.[31] (If this means that she resorted to contraception – see the fascinating article in the *Oxford Classical Dictionary*[32] – it tells us that her union with him was not a *mariage blanc*.) And, according to the *HA*, her husband asserted that, if he had been a private citizen he would have divorced her, so moody and shrewish was she.[33] Matters came to a head when Hadrian dismissed a significant number of officials 'for behaving in a more familiar manner towards Sabina than court etiquette demanded'.[34] Among those ousted was his chief secretary Suetonius whose access to the imperial archives enabled him to compose his lives of the Caesars and of the poet Horace. The fact that her husband had cut her adrift from the courtiers whom she presumably found sympathetic will have fanned the flames of Sabina's hatred still further.

Rebuilding Rome

A famous story tells how the 30-year-old Julius Caesar came to Gades (Cadiz) in Further Spain and saw a statue of Alexander the Great in the temple of Hercules. He let out a groan at the thought that he himself had done nothing memorable at the age when Alexander had already conquered the world.[1] If Hadrian had ever been prey to such emotions, Trajan's disastrous expansionist policy had certainly educated him out of them. He was much respected, however, as a military man. The *HA* informs us that 'though he desired peace rather than war, he trained the soldiers as if war were imminent, instilling into them the example of his own endurance'.[2] He led a soldier's life among the troops and was happy to eat the same food as them out in the open with them. He inspired others by the example of his own spirit, walking as much as 32 kilometres fully armed. As we have seen, he set himself against traces of luxury in the camps; he himself often wore the humblest clothing. Above all, discipline was his watchword. The *HA* suggests that this had grown slack since Augustus' day and the importance Hadrian put on it is hammered home by the striking of coins celebrating the 'Emperor's Discipline'.[3] If the troops knew about his homosexuality, they doubtless laughed it off, as Julius Caesar's men had done over his purported fling with Nicomedes, king of Bithynia.[4]

But it is no accident that we think of Hadrian above all else as the builder of some of the empire's finest structures. He was passionate about architecture and no doubt saw that great buildings stood a chance of providing a more lasting legacy than evanescent conquests.

As the *HA* remarks, 'he built something in almost every city', and, in the same vein, Fronto comments that one can 'see memorials of his journeys erected in most cities of Asia and Europe'.[5] As one travels the Roman world, one feels like echoing the inscription in St Paul's Cathedral for Sir Christopher Wren: 'If you seek a monument, look about you'. In addition, as Opper points out, the building activity not only stimulated employment but also strengthened the cohesion of the empire, especially in the east.[6] Building materials such as marble and precious stones came from all over its vast expanse. At the same time, buildings in the provinces reflected those in the capital. Roman architecture gave a unity to an empire that covered enormous stretches of three continents.

The massive spoils from the Dacian wars made a hugely ambitious building programme in Rome a viable possibility. Trajan had led the way here with the magnificent Forum designed by his architect Apollodorus, and his column, baths and markets. Hadrian no doubt set out to surpass him, and he succeeded, his projects inevitably continuing the boost in employment opportunities generated by his predecessor.

The most dazzling survivor among Hadrian's buildings is the Pantheon, his great temple of all the gods, set at the heart of Rome and still in a miraculous state of preservation thanks to its use as a Christian church (Santa Maria ad Martyres) from 609 AD. It is covered by the largest un-reinforced concrete dome in the world. This dome, crowned by a 9-metre-wide hole known as the *oculus* (eye) at its centre to let in the light as well as the rain and snow, takes the breath away with its perfect geometry and its awesome spatial volume. It contains five horizontal rings of 28 coffers each, every coffer sprouting bronze rosettes (all alas now lost) and thus furnishing a gleaming canopy which reminded Dio Cassius of the heavens.[7] Indeed a cosmological dimension has often been identified in the Pantheon's architecture.[8]

Figure 9   The dome of the Pantheon

There are inconsistencies between the alignment of the noble porch and the domed rotunda.[9] (It seems that the original design called for even bigger columns, but this had to be modified because not enough of them could be supplied.) Even so, the result is profoundly impressive. In a memorable scene from Peter Greenaway's film *The Belly of an Architect*, a party consisting of the architect and fellow professionals having dinner outside a restaurant opposite the floodlit façade of the Pantheon rise to their feet to applaud it.

The materials from which the Pantheon was built provide a classic illustration of how the resources of the whole empire were called into play.[10] The outer columns supporting the portico are of grey granite from Mons Claudianus in Upper Egypt, while the inner two rows are of rose granite from Aswan. Porphyry came from Mons Porphyrius in Egypt, other materials from Ionia, Numidia (Tunisia), Phrygia, the Peloponnese and Thessaly. White marble came from Attica, the Proconnesos (an island in the Sea of Marmara) and Luna (in Etruria).

Figure 10 The Pantheon

The transportation of the great monolithic shafts of the columns proved a considerable challenge for Roman technology. The 15-metre shafts, weighing some 90 tonnes, from Mons Claudianus had to be transported some 100 kilometres through the desert of Upper Egypt to the Nile. Here they were loaded onto special barges and then, in the Nile delta, trans-shipped onto huge sea-going vessels, stone transports specially constructed for the purpose. It is tempting to believe that their arrival in Rome and their erection on site sparked lively public interest.

However, the key element in this vast structure was none of these splendid materials; it was the concrete already mentioned in the context of the dome. The invention of this substance was one of Rome's major contributions to the world. Towards the end of the third century BC, it had been discovered that mixing lime, water and a gritty substance such as sand produces on setting a cohesive and tough material well adapted to bonding masonry and serving as a building material in itself. Its triumphant use in 174 BC in the *Porticus Aemilia*, a huge warehouse in the river-port of Rome, opened the way to countless large-scale building projects as the Romans became increasingly skilled in its use. Most spectacularly, concrete vaults were able to achieve much greater spans than in previous constructions and this made possible the creation of vast internal spaces, as in the great bathing halls of Caracalla and Diocletian of the third and fourth centuries AD.[11] If you are in Rome, you will find that the Church of Santa Maria degli Angeli off the Piazza della Repubblica well repays a visit. It is Michelangelo's adaptation (of 1563 to 66) of the nucleus of the central bathing block of Diocletian's baths. Though damagingly refashioned some 200 years later, it still gives a breathtaking impression of the space achievable in these concrete buildings. The use of the new material perhaps attained its apogee in two of Hadrian's most ambitious projects: the Pantheon in the city and the landscaped complex of his villa at Tivoli.

There had been two previous Pantheons on the site, both of which had fallen victim to fire, and, with becoming modesty, Hadrian repeated on the architrave the original dedicating inscription to Marcus Agrippa, Augustus' great general and son-in-law, who built the first, probably in 27 or 25 BC.

Altogether less modest was the use to which Hadrian put the building. He held court there, giving public audiences and sitting on a tribunal surrounded by his foremost advisors.[12] As Opper remarks, 'the huge celestial dome set the emperor into an almost cosmological framework'.[13] It has recently been argued that the positioning of the *oculus* means that at midday during the March equinox and on 21 April, the traditional founding date of Rome, the sunbeam strikes the doorway (on the equinox) and a metal grill above it (on 21 April), in the latter case flooding the porch outside with light.[14] If Hadrian had timed his entry at this point, he would have been illuminated as if by studio lights. These moments of high theatre, in which the sun god spotlit the emperor as he came into the temple that he had built with wondrous materials from all over his empire, must have created an overwhelmingly powerful impression.

The building has been the victim of subsequent depredations, most famously those of Urban VIII, a seventeenth-century pope from the Barberini family – a fact which led to the celebrated pasquinade, 'Quod non fecerunt barbari, fecerunt Barberini' (What the barbarians didn't do, the Barberini made up for). Yet it remains astonishing.

A nineteenth-century impression

In his poem *Childe Harold's Pilgrimage*, Lord Byron describes the Pantheon, in his day a Christian church containing the tombs of great Italians:

Simple, erect, severe, austere, sublime –
Shrine of all saints and temple of all gods,
From Jove to Jesus – spared and blest by time;
Looking tranquillity, while falls or nods
Arch, empire, each thing round thee, and man plods
His way through thorns to ashes – glorious dome!
Shalt thou not last? Time's scythes and tyrants' rods
Shiver upon thee – sanctuary and home
Of art and piety – Pantheon! – pride of Rome![15]

Hadrian's next – and even larger – architectural project was the temple of the goddess Venus and Rome. The building was seriously damaged by a fire in 307 AD, and what can be seen now are the remains of the substantially different rebuilding by Maxentius, a later emperor. However, we can state with certainty that Hadrian's temple, built on a substructure designed by Apollodorus, incorporated important Greek elements, derived especially from the vast temple of Olympian Zeus in Athens. The mouldings of the temple's entablature appear to be influenced by buildings in Asia Minor, further in the Greek east. In this building, Hadrian projected himself as the new Romulus, Rome's founder, and it is significant that he chose to build a Greek temple for this purpose. Hadrian was making a Roman statement in the centre of the city but setting it in a Greek context.

Figure 11 Hadrian. © Trustees of the British Museum

We shall return to this in our discussion of the *Graeculus* and Athens in Chapter 9.

Immense changes were being wrought in the cityscape. The temple was built over the vestibule of Nero's notorious Domus Aurea, and Nero's great colossus, a bronze statue of himself some 30 to 40 metres in height, was removed, its features having been replaced in the reign of Vespasian with those of the sun god Helios. Twenty-four elephants under the supervision of the architect Decrianus were needed to effect the removal.[16] Hadrian spent little time in Rome, but Mary Boatwright is right to remark that his effect on the city was profound: 'he permanently changed the urban landscape and touched all segments of the population.'[17]

Figure 2.1 (caption illegible)

Hadrian's Villa – the Sunny Pleasure Dome and the Caves of Ice

A creation quite as memorable as the great structures Hadrian built in Rome was 28 kilometres – half a day's ride – from the city. This was his villa at Tivoli, the largest known from the Roman world.[1] Its scale is overwhelming. We know of some 900 rooms and corridors, but there were many more of both. The grounds probably covered at least 120 hectares. At this location, the public business of the empire was transacted, but it was also a private playground for the emperor and his guests. As Opper illuminatingly puts it, 'the villa appears like a mixture between the splendid extravagance of Versailles combined with the purposeful informality of a large English country house'.[2]

Hadrian's character was ideally suited to the management of this huge project. Aurelius Victor tells us that 'on the example of the military legions, he had mustered into cohorts workmen, stone-masons, architects, and every type of specialist for the building and decorating of the walls'.[3] But even while the building operation was managed with staggering military efficiency, an extraordinary creative ambition and originality found supreme expression. The most up-to-date construction techniques were pushed to their very limits, as, for instance, in the villa's proliferation of domes. (We shall soon see that the architect Apollodorus mocked Hadrian's obsession with what he referred to scornfully as 'pumpkins'). The architectural rule book of Vitruvius from the first century BC was ripped up. Characterized by an extraordinary opulence from its greatest structures to its frescoes and inlays of multicoloured marble tiles, the villa is a fantastic amalgam of contrasting shapes and irregularities. It makes a statement, but its bold modernism sets it apart from other great propagandist structures. As Opper remarks, 'It is this supreme confidence in the inspiring persuasiveness of the utterly unconventional that projects an almost modern sense of leadership in strong contrast to the monumental façades, strict symmetry and absurdly exaggerated scale employed by other regimes before and since.'[4]

As for the overall design, the *HA* tells us that:

> He built the villa at Tivoli in so wonderful a way that he called sections
> of it by the most famous names of the provinces and sites, such as the
> Lyceum, the Academy, the Prytaneum [all in Athens], the Canopus
> [on the Nile delta], the Poikile [an art gallery in Athens] and the Vale
> of Tempe [in Thessaly], and – so that he shouldn't leave anything out
> – he even created an underworld.[5]

Hadrian was in fact following in the footsteps of previous wealthy villa owners such as Cicero in naming areas of an estate after

Figure 12   Hadrian's Villa

celebrated classical sites, but it is clear in Hadrian's case that this feature of the design reflected his wide travels and that the site was what Diana Spencer calls 'a synecdoche for empire', the decidedly upmarket Disneyland or Las Vegas of its day.[6] A plethora of sculptures showcased copies of the great masterpieces of Greek art of the fifth and fourth centuries BC, of famous Hellenistic works and of Egyptian figures. Greek philosophers, orators and statesmen found their place too amid a vast range of portrayals. In addition to large-scale lakes, pools and canals, a sophisticated hydraulic system operated a huge array of watercourses and fountains (the inspiration for those in the gardens of the sixteenth-century Villa d'Este up the hill in Tivoli itself). Today, tourist guides point enthusiastically to the so-called Maritime Theatre, possibly the private apartment of the emperor on an artificial island surrounded by a circular moat.[7] There were two removable wooden bridges which could, they claim, be taken away when the emperor wished to remain totally undisturbed. It sounds like paradise on earth, and it comes as a surprise to be told

Figure 13 The Maritime Theatre at Hadrian's Villa

by the philosopher Philostratos that Hadrian's favourite villa was not
this, but the one at Antium.[8]

On the personal side, Dio Cassius gives an alarming account of the
relations between Hadrian and the architect Apollodorus:

> Hadrian first banished and then put to death the architect Apollodorus,
> who had built the projects of Trajan in Rome, the forum, the odeon
> and the gymnasium. The pretext was that he had committed some
> offence, but the real reason was that when Trajan was consulting
> him about some aspect of the buildings and Hadrian broke in with
> some remark, he said to him, 'Go away and draw your pumpkins.
> You understand nothing of these matters.' (Hadrian at that point
> happened to be very proud of one of his drawings.) And so, when
> he became emperor, Hadrian remembered this insult and could not
> endure his freedom of speech. He sent him the plan of the temple
> of Venus and Rome in order to show him that a great work could be
> accomplished without him, and he asked him whether the design was
> good. Apollodorus replied with regard to the temple that it should
> have been built on high ground and the earth should have been dug
> away beneath it so that it would have been more conspicuous on the
> Sacred Way from a higher position and it could have accommodated
> the machines in the hollowed-out part, so that they could be fitted
> together unobserved and brought into the theatre without anyone
> realizing before; and with regard to the statues, he replied that they
> had been made too tall in proportion to the height of the *cella*. 'For
> now,' he said, 'if the goddesses wish to get up and go out, they won't be
> able to.' Since he had written this so frankly, Hadrian was angry and
> extremely upset that he had fallen into an error that could not be put
> right, and he restrained neither his anger nor his grief, but killed him.[9]

The anecdote, unsupported by any corroborating evidence, gives us a
picture of a vindictively tyrannical Hadrian that simply does not square
with what we know about him. Furthermore, while there is nothing to
show that Apollodorus participated in the design or building of the villa,
he was, as we have seen, involved in the Pantheon and Temple of Venus
and Rome projects. In addition, his critique about the goddesses seems

scarcely serious. The same would apply to Pheidias' great gold and ivory statue of Zeus in the temple at Olympia, and *that* was one of the seven wonders of the ancient world. While it is not difficult to believe in tensions between the amateur and professional architect, it seems sensible to side with the many scholars who dismiss the story's historicity.[10] If the part of it that records Apollodorus' mockery of Hadrian's doodles of pumpkin-like domes is true, we can at least conclude that the builder of the Pantheon and the multi-domed villa had the last laugh.

To keep the enormous complex that was Hadrian's villa functioning, a vast slave force was a necessity. However, underground staff passages, traced to a length of 4.8 kilometres, ensured that their activity was largely unseen by the emperor and his guests. This separation is strikingly illustrated in the so-called Cento Camerelle where slaves' tenement housing blocks up to 12 metres high were built at a lower level than one of the main access roads for official visitors and separated from the road by a screen wall.

We can only guess at how these slaves were treated, though the tombs of some of them, including Hadrian's old wet nurse Germana, along the villa's perimeter are evidence that these ones at least were appreciated. It is nevertheless hard not to feel misgivings about a building – and indeed a society – that was so dependent on slave labour.

Slaves are the victims of appalling injustice, but before we make too harsh judgments on the past, we should remember that slavery was not abolished in the British Empire until 1833, nor in the USA until 1863; until the eighteenth century, it was taken for granted. The fact that people-trafficking operates on a large scale in the modern world denies us the right to an easy complacency, though at least it is now illegal.

Many slaves in the Roman world had been defeated in warfare and their conquerors could have killed them. As a result, they and their children were supposed to feel gratitude, and there was a spurious logic to the fact that they had no rights at all. In fact, however, slaves came from other sources as well. Many were the victims of

kidnapping or piracy; many were unwanted children who had either
been left out to die – the word for this is exposed – by their parents
at birth and then rescued, or been sold off to slave-traders when they
were older. Slavery was big business and it is said that at one of its
main centres, the Greek island of Delos in the middle of the Aegean,
10,000 slaves could be sold in a day.[11]

Conditions for slaves varied considerably. Those who rowed in the
galleys or worked in the mines, quarries or vast country estates endured
a grim existence. Literate and intelligent slaves had some chance of
avoiding these fates. The best situation was to be born in a household
where you might be treated, up to a point, as one of the family, for the
Roman *familia* included the slaves: this may have led to a sense that they
actually belonged somewhere. Legally, however, slaves had no individual
rights. Masters gave them their names and addressed the males of
whatever age as *puer* (boy). They could punish without fear of the law.
Vedius Pollio ordered a boy who had broken a precious crystal cup to be
executed by being thrown to the lampreys in his fish pond.[12] (Augustus
got him off.) The doctor Galen tells the story of a friend of his who
discovered on a journey that two slave-boys had left behind a case he
particularly wanted. He took a sword in its scabbard and beat them about
the head so passionately that the blade split the sheath and the boys were
horribly injured.[13] Hadrian himself flew into a rage with his secretary and
poked out his eye.[14] (When the repentant Hadrian asked him to request
a gift, he eventually replied that all he wanted was to get his eye back.)
Cato the Elder, the classic old-school Roman, recommended that sick
and old slaves should be sold off, not kept on unproductively.[15] Even if
slaves and freedmen often gave each other emotional support, and those
who had a reasonably close relationship with their master could expect
to be freed, the fact remains that their situation was extremely insecure.
They could be beaten, sold or killed, though the last *would* lead to trouble
with the authorities, and Hadrian, in line with his generally thoughtful
and humane legislation, specifically forbade it.[16]

Some masters, however, treated their slaves very well. The philosopher Seneca wrote to a friend:

> I am delighted to discover from some people who have come from
> seeing you that you live on friendly terms with your slaves. This is
> what I should have expected of your good sense and learning. People
> say, 'They are slaves.' I disagree. They are men. 'They are slaves,' they
> say. No, they are people you share your house with. 'They are slaves.'
> No, they are fellow-slaves if you reflect how much power fortune has
> over both slaves and free alike ... Consider that the man you call a
> slave is born from the same species as yourself, enjoys the same sky,
> and lives, breathes and dies just as you do.[17]

Such enlightened platitudes cannot disguise the fact that nobody – and certainly not the nascent Christian Church – thought of freeing all their slaves. They should perhaps be balanced by a picture of slaves working in a mill from Apuleius' *Golden Ass*, a novel from the second century AD. The writing may well be hyperbolical, but the unhygienized description has an authentic ring of truth:

> As to the human contingent – what a crew! – their whole bodies
> pricked out with livid weals, their whip-scarred backs shaded rather
> than covered by their tattered rags, some with only a scanty loin-cloth
> by way of covering, and all of them showing through the rents in what
> clothes they had. There were branded foreheads, half-shaven heads,
> and fettered ankles; their faces were sallow, their eyes so bleared by the
> smoky heat of the furnaces that they were half blind; and like boxers,
> who sprinkle themselves with dust before fighting, they were dirty
> white all over with a floury powder.[18]

Here is a true glimpse into hell. Hadrian's villa is certainly a monument to high civilization as well as self-indulgent luxury, but we should not allow ourselves to forget the Romans' often grim and frequently brutish treatment of the underclass which was the motor that powered their world.

Bread and Circuses – Keeping the People Happy

As we have seen, Hadrian gave inspirational leadership to his soldiers. But what was it necessary for an emperor to do to get Rome's civilian population on his side? Courting popularity by providing civic amenities such as baths and laying on public entertainments was often seen by emperors as a vital ingredient in their security, amply justifying any amount of expenditure; and Hadrian was no exception to this general rule. The satirist Juvenal, Hadrian's contemporary, remarked that the people 'had an anxious desire for two things only, bread and circuses.'[1] Though he might well have added their addiction to public bathing (which we shall go on to explore shortly), he hits the nail devastatingly on the head. Free grain was available to those adult male citizens resident in Rome whose names were on an official list entitling them to tickets which could be exchanged for the corn dole.[2] Woe betide an emperor who could not guarantee regular food supplies! But the need to mix with – or at least be seen by – the people was equally paramount. The baths, the races and the bloody shows in the Colosseum gave Hadrian the opportunity to burnish the imperial image on both a small and a large scale.

While their baths were indeed an impressive feature of the Romans' experience, it is important not to view their advances in hygiene in too idealizing a manner. Reg in *Monty Python's Life of Brian* asks the challenging question, 'All right, but apart from the sanitation, medicine, education, wine, public order, irrigation, roads, the fresh water system and public health, *what* have the Romans ever done for us?' This inverted tribute to Roman civilization does in its comic way give some idea of the benefits it gave to the empire. Tacitus may have written scathingly of the corrupting influence of Roman baths on the Britons (see p.29) but, generally speaking, the rise in the standard of living the Romans brought with them must have been a significant factor in the acquiescence in their rule. We know that in Trajan's day, Rome's famous water system, which had been given its first clean-up in 34 to 33 BC by Agrippa (the builder of the original Pantheon), brought some 1,500 litres of fresh water per hour into the city day and night, and was clearly extremely beneficial for public health.[3] Communal public lavatories could look very grand. The seats were built over a deep drain which carried rain or fountain water while fresh water flowed through a gutter in front of the seats. In these those relieving themselves, seated in rows with an extraordinary lack of privacy, would dip sponges on sticks to wipe themselves. It is difficult to believe that the water was able to wash away all the excrement. There were some luxuriously appointed private lavatories in the houses of the wealthy, but they must have been little more than cesspits. At least the most upmarket ones in Hadrian's villa had splendid views over the surrounding countryside.

Whether or not he utilized the public lavatories, Hadrian certainly took an interest in the baths, one of the most distinctive features of Roman civilization. In the city, he restored the Baths of Agrippa and created separate baths for men and women.[4] And he often bathed in the public baths 'with all and sundry'.[5] Yet a question mark must remain over just how healthy these baths were. How effectively did the water circulate, if at all? Gastric disease was common; if you went to the baths with an open wound, you got gangrene,[6] and the plain of the Tiber remained malarial until the present river embankments were built in the early twentieth century.[7] Rome was not a healthy city – it stank from the presence of so vast a population[8] – and many a Roman could have exclaimed along with the poet Horace, 'O countryside, when shall I see you!'[9] There were further disadvantages to the bath-houses. Seneca, the philosopher and playwright of the first century BC, describes the drawbacks of living over one.[10] The weightlifters puff and pant. The masseurs noisily slap their customers. The ball-players count their throws out loud. There's a hubbub as a clothes stealer or a shoplifter is caught. The man who likes the sound of his own voice sings in the bath. People leap into the pool with a great splash. The depilator advertises his services with a nasal whine when he is not making his customers howl as he plucks out their hairs. Then there are the cries of the drinks-vendor, the sausage-seller, the pie-seller and all the tavern salesmen. One hopes that the baths Hadrian frequented were not plagued with this cacophonous ensemble!

Another famous feature of ancient Rome was the blood-stained staging of gladiatorial fights and wild-beast hunts in the amphi-theatre. Hadrian was a zealous addict of this grisly carnage.[11] He presented games in nearly every city; he put on a hunt of a thousand wild beasts in the stadium at Athens; in the Circus Maximus in Rome, he had many wild beasts and often a hundred lions slaughtered.[12]

In a well-known letter, Seneca describes his distaste when he arrived at the games at midday as condemned criminals were being forced to fight each other.[13] (Wild beast hunts usually took place in the morning, gladiatorial combats in the afternoon. The lunch break could feature some supposedly light entertainment.)

It so happened that I stumbled on the games at midday, hoping for entertainment and for some relaxation in which men's eyes could take a rest from human blood. It was quite the opposite. All the previous fighting was tender-hearted in comparison: now it was sheer butchery in earnest. They have nothing to cover them: their whole bodies exposed to blows, they never strike in vain … There are no helmets, no shields to beat off the swords … 'But,' someone will say, 'one of them committed robbery with violence and killed a man.' So what? Because he killed, does he deserve to suffer this: and you, what did you do

Figure 14   Gladiators (Villa Borghese, Rome)

to deserve to watch this? 'You attendants, kill them, lash them burn them! Why is he rushing into his opponent's sword so timidly? Why is he dying in such a cowardly way? Drive him amid the wounds! ... There's an interval in the games. Let men be murdered to fill the gap!'

We shall clearly share Seneca's disgust at humans, as Lord Byron put it, being 'Butcher'd to make a Roman holiday',[14] but ancient audiences, including the supposedly civilized Greeks, undisguisedly relished such brutality. In a striking chapter of his *Confessions*, St Augustine says that a friend of his went to the games and found 'the whole place growing hot with the most monstrous joy'.[15] He had entered with strong feelings of resistance, but was then caught up in the general frenzy and became an addict. In their lively book *The Colosseum*, Keith Hopkins and Mary Beard rightly dub Seneca an oddball[16] and though they go on to quote the tax authorities of 177 AD as arguing that the treasury 'should not be stained with the splashing of human blood' and that it was morally offensive to get money from what was 'forbidden by all laws of gods and humans', such fastidiousness will have been rare indeed.[17]

Massive slaughter for mass audiences had long been a great Roman tradition.[18] In the first century BC, Caesar's leading opponent Pompey laid on some 20 elephants, 600 lions and 410 leopards, and other beasts in addition. In his autobiography, Augustus proudly proclaimed that he had killed off a total of 3,500 animals in African beast hunts in the course of his reign, including 36 crocodiles on one occasion. We must hope that one late Roman historian was fantasizing when he tells us that the late third-century emperor laid on 'a thousand ostriches, a thousand stags, then ibexes, wild-sheep and other herbivores'. It comes as something of a relief to discover that there was one occasion in 55 BC when the elephants being stabbed to death with spears aroused a degree of sympathy from the spectators 'and a feeling that there was a certain fellowship between that beast and the human race'.[19]

In 80 AD, the Colosseum, that great theatre of death, was inaugurated with a hundred-day orgy of fighting. (Hopkins and Beard helpfully advise that, if you are flying in to Ciampino airport south of Rome, you should sit by a right-hand window, as there is an

Figure 15   The Colosseum

impressive view of the spectacular remains as you cross the city. And as I write this, £20 million is being spent on the building's restoration.)[20] Romans would dress smartly in their togas for the slaughter, cramming themselves into one of the 50,000-odd seats. The awnings to ward against the heat of the Roman sun could not have covered more than half the amphitheatre, so those in the grandest seats by the arena would roast.[21] It wasn't just mad dogs and Englishmen who went out in the midday sun! As we have seen, the Colosseum wasn't the only location for the games in Rome, but it must have given a huge impetus to the grisly dances of death. Emperors and ambitious politicians could win considerable prestige through extravagance

A horrific myth becomes real in the Colosseum

The great games which inaugurated the Colosseum were celebrated in a series of epigrams by the Spanish poet Martial. Convicts, with an unspecified crime taken for granted, were executed in ghastly real-life enactments of ancient myths. Here the fate of Prometheus, whose innards were constantly devoured by an eagle and as constantly renewed so that the torture imposed on him by Zeus would never cease, is literally but perversely enacted on the condemned Laureolus. The myth had been the subject of plays. Now it is real:

> Just as Prometheus, bound on the Scythian crag, fed the unremitting bird with his all too expansive chest, so did Laureolus expose his bare flesh to a Caledonian boar as he hung on a cross that was very real. His lacerated joints lived on as his limbs dribbled blood, and though there was a body there, you couldn't see it. He finally met with the punishment he deserved. The guilty man had dug into the throat of his father or of his master with his sword, or in his madness had despoiled a temple of its secret store of gold or had laid a savage torch, Rome, to you. The criminal had outdone the crimes of the ancient story. In him what had been a play was an execution. [23]

in putting on games. Those that Hadrian staged before becoming emperor cost two million sesterces.[22]

Another famous Roman sport – think *Ben Hur* – was chariot racing, and this fits the template of modern sporting enthusiasm far more than the blood-stained games we have just described. The aristocratic Pliny wrote to a friend expressing his view of the races with a contemptuous hauteur.[24] (Somewhat surprisingly, he did not seem to have the same problem with gladiatorial shows.)[25] The shirts he refers to were red, white, green and blue and marked out which of Rome's four clubs of racers each belonged to:

> I have spent all this time among my writing tablets and papers in the most delightful peace and quiet. 'How could you,' you will say, 'in the city?' The races were on, a type of spectacle which does not hold even the slightest attraction for me. There's no novelty, no variety – once seen is quite enough. So I am all the more surprised that so many thousands of grown men should have such a childish desire to see galloping horses and men standing in their chariots again and again. If they were attracted by the speed of the horses or the skill of the drivers, there would at least be some reason for it; as it is they support a shirt, they care passionately about a shirt and, if the colours were to be changed around in mid-course in a race, their enthusiasm and loyalty would change too, and they would suddenly abandon the famous riders and the famous horses whose name they shout when they recognize them at a distance. There is so much popularity, so much importance in a single utterly worthless shirt – I don't mean with the crowd, which is even more worthless than the shirt, but with certain perfectly serious men. When I reflect that they sit there never getting enough of a pointless and boring activity, I take some pleasure in the fact that I am not attracted by the pleasure myself. And it is with the greatest pleasure that I am spending my time on literary work during the days which others are wasting in the most futile of occupations.

Hadrian certainly attended the races,[26] thus qualifying as one of Pliny's serious men whom he regards as so conspicuously wasting their time. He did not wish to stand aloof from the common people of Rome and he would have frequented the city's two great racecourses, the Circus Maximus (capacity 250,000) and the smaller Circus of Gaius and Nero, to watch such racing stars as Appuleius Diocles, a Spaniard from Lusitania, who ran in more than 4,000 races and won 1,500 of them, gaining a total of 35,863,120 sesterces.[27] Pliny has a remarkable ability to enrage his readers, who find his particular brand of complacency repulsive. For my part, I generally admire him for his decency, generosity and shrewdness, but I have to part company with him here. Chariot racing won plaudits in Homer's *Iliad* and Rome's great epic, Virgil's *Aeneid*, and was a staple of the Olympic games. It was also highly dangerous, calling for considerable courage. It *was* to appreciate the drivers' expertise as well as to enjoy the thrills and spills that people flocked to the races: betting was illegal, though it certainly happened.[28] If modern horse racing is the sport of kings, why should an ancient equivalent not have been the sport of the emperor Hadrian? And in any case, attendance at the races was one of the things expected of an emperor. His appearance there was, as we have seen, a vital part of his imperial image.

8

The Journeys

Anthony R. Birley subtitles his excellent full-dress biography of Hadrian 'the restless emperor', justly remarking that his prolonged provincial tours are the most obvious feature of his reign.[1] The man who devoted so much time and thought to his villa at Tivoli in fact spent comparatively little time there, apparently preferring to travel the vast tracts of the Roman world. The writer Annaeus Florus teased him about his obsessive journeying in a lampoon:

> I don't want to be Caesar, please
> – To tramp round the Britons, weak at the knees,
> In the Scythian frosts to freeze. [2]

The emperor replied in equally playful vein:

> I don't want to be Florus, please,
> To tramp round pubs, into bars to squeeze,
> To lurk about eating pies and peas,
> To get myself infested with fleas.

Wanderlust was clearly deep in Hadrian's bones.

In our days of easy travel, it is perhaps difficult to appreciate quite how remarkable Hadrian's journeying was. Although the Roman army created massive mobility throughout the empire, its rulers normally just didn't do this sort of thing. They sat in Rome and, if they travelled, it was for military reasons. For the overwhelming majority of provincials, a glimpse of Hadrian in the flesh would have been more than a once-in-a-lifetime experience. Their generation would be uniquely blessed.

We have already taken Hadrian to Germany, Africa and Britain and we shall discuss his visits to Athens and other parts of Greece in the next chapter. When he left Britain in 122 AD after the building of the wall, he continued through Gaul to Spain, then went on to Syria, Cappadocia, Bithynia, Asia, Greece and Sicily. The *HA* gives us some tantalizing glimpses of these travels:

> At this same time he built a temple of wonderful workmanship in honour of Plotina [Trajan's empress] at Nîmes. After this he made for the provinces of Spain and spent the winter at Tarragona where he restored the temple of Augustus at his own expense ... At this time he fell into very great danger – which in fact won him glory. As he was walking about in a garden at Tarragona, a slave of his host rushed at him madly with a sword. He simply took hold of him and handed him over to the servants when they ran up. When it was discovered that he was mad, he passed him to the doctors for treatment. He never showed a flicker of alarm.
>
> Afterwards he sailed to Sicily where he climbed Mount Etna to see the sunrise, which they say is many-coloured like a rainbow. From there he went to Rome and from there he crossed over to Africa and bestowed many kindnesses on the African provinces. Hardly any emperor covered so much territory with so much speed.[3]

Another round of travel in 128 to 132, to which we shall return later, took Hadrian to Africa, Greece, Asia, Syria, Palmyra, Arabia, Judaea, Egypt, Syria, Thrace, Moesia and Greece again. As usual, he commemorated his sojourns with a series of coins which depicted himself greeting the appropriate province, the latter being portrayed as an idealized female form marked out by some local attribute (Egypt, for example, being shown with a large basket of grain and an ibis).[4] It is scarcely surprising that the *HA* remarks of him that 'he was so fond of travelling that he wanted to inform himself by personal experience of everything which he had read about the different parts of the world'.[5] The *HA* adds the information that 'he put up with cold and bad weather with such endurance that he never covered his head' (see the description by Dio Cassius in Chapter 3, p.20).[6] Clearly, Hadrian had the committed traveller's hardy constitution.

Hadrian will have travelled in a manner befitting an emperor. In his train, there followed an *agmen comitantium* (a column of companions), consisting of the men of the Praetorian Guard, his Batavian bodyguard and his troops of all kinds of experts in the construction and decoration of great buildings.[7] In addition, there was his secretarial staff. Considerable preparation and mastery of logistics would be vital to ensure the success of his visits.[8] We have an inscription from Palmyra (in Syria) recording that a city clerk called Males provided food for the citizens and the influx of visitors and saw to the reception of the army during a visit by Hadrian in 130 AD.[9] As for lengthy preparation, we possess a letter from a village secretary listing provisions 'for the presence of the greatest Emperor Hadrian' in Alexandria; they include barley, hay, suckling-pigs, dates, full-grown pigs, sheep, oil, chaff and olives. The letter is dated 19 December 129 and Hadrian arrived in August of the next year.[10]

Such imperial visits were not always going to prove altogether welcome to the local inhabitants; but in his extravagant panegyric to the emperor Trajan, Pliny holds him up as a model guest. With him there was 'no disturbance in requisitioning vehicles, no fastidiousness about *hospitia* (accommodation); he had the same supplies as others.'[11] Pliny contrasts this with the journeys of Domitian – 'if indeed they were journeys rather than devastations'. Hadrian's successor Antoninus Pius refused to visit the provinces at all on the grounds that an imperial train inevitably imposed a burden on the provincials.[12] On the other hand, as we have noted, an emperor's arrival could create enormous excitement in an empire, vast tracts of which regarded him as a god. Mamertinus recounts the visit of two of the four emperors to Milan in the winter of 290 to 291 AD:

All the fields were filled with crowds not only of men rushing to see, but with herds of beasts leaving their remote pastures and woods; the peasants vied with each other in reporting what they had seen to all the villages. Altars were lit, incense thrown on, libations poured, sacrificial victims slain.[13]

The enthusiasm of the animals for the tetrarchs' arrival highlights the hyperbole of Mamertinus' panegyric, but surely does not subvert its essential enthusiasm.

We know of no adverse local comments on Hadrian's visits. This may have been in part because the provincials were surely not slow to understand his consistent policy of fostering civic life throughout the empire and his eagerness to pour money into the project. Furthermore, an ecstatic welcome would have made him more likely to grant privileges in return. The emperor's presence, which would be viewed as the epiphany of a god, strengthened the reciprocal bond between the supplicating city and the beneficent ruler. The imperial cult proliferated, not simply on a provincial and municipal basis, but on a personal one too, as is evidenced by the hundreds of small altars dedicated to Hadrian, possibly for household sacrifices along the emperor's route.

On a more down-to-earth level, access to the emperor was comparatively easy on the journeys. It is possible that only a single example of an emperor failing to grant a request is recorded. This was when Vespasian's son Titus – not unsurprisingly in view of his notorious sack of Jerusalem in 70 AD – refused a petition of the citizens of Antioch to expel the Jews or cancel their civic privileges.[14] (Titus had by now destroyed Jerusalem – see Chapter 11 – and told the people of Antioch only too accurately that there was nowhere else for the Jews to go.)[15] A famous story recounted by Dio Cassius tellingly illustrates Hadrian's attitude. On one of his journeys, a woman approached him with a request. At first he told her that he didn't have the time. She riposted, 'Then stop being emperor!' He turned round and listened to what she had to say.[16]

Hadrian's travels thus served the same kind of bonding purpose as the famous 'progresses' of Queen Elizabeth I and the journeys of Britain's present royal family. We must now consider the benefits they brought on the ground to the cities visited. For this purpose, we shall discuss the building programmes he inaugurated in three of the cities he visited: Smyrna in Ionia, Cyzicus in Mysia and Cyrene in Africa.

Hadrian's love of Greek philosophy predisposed him to lend a sympathetic ear to the pleas of the philosopher and orator Marcus Antonius Polemon to show favour to Smyrna. In his *Lives of the Sophists*, Philostratos tells us that that Polemon had attended Smyrna's celebrated schools of rhetoric as a youth and that

> he was of great value to the city in going on embassies to the emperors and defending its traditions. For example, he converted Hadrian, who had previously favoured the Ephesians, to the Smyrnaeans' side to such an extent that in one day Hadrian poured out ten million drachmas on Smyrna, from which the grain market was built, as well as the most magnificent gymnasium in Asia and a temple that can be seen from afar.[17]

An inscription preserves part of a list of private and public donors to the gymnasium complex in Smyrna, a basilica with bronze doors, a columned anointing room with a gilt roof, a porticoed palm court with gardens and a temple of Tyche (Chance).[18] Among other gifts, Hadrian contributed columns for the anointing room. Here we see in operation Hadrian's policy of stimulating civic and private contributions to local building schemes through his own generosity. He was also showing honour to Polemon, whom he subsequently took with him on his travels. The philosopher may not have been an entirely problem-free addition to his retinue, however. An aristocrat as well as an intellectual, Polemon 'aroused criticism, because when he travelled he was followed by a long train of baggage-animals, with many horses, servants and dogs of various breeds for different kinds of hunting. He himself used to ride in a Phrygian or Celtic carriage, with silver-mounted bridles.'[19]

Figure 16 The basilica in the agora of Smyrna (photo: Peter Thonemann)

His passion for hunting, however, would have made him all the more agreeable as a travelling companion for Hadrian.

Philostratos may have been mistaken, incidentally, in saying that Polemon steered Hadrian's patronage away from Ephesus, a city he visited on at least two and probably more of his journeys through the East.[20] In 124 AD, he listened 'with pleasure' to the ephebes (boys advancing into adulthood) singing his praises in the theatre. And, possibly on his way back from his final journey in 131, he awarded Ephesus its second provincial temple.[21]

We now move on to Cyzicus, a city in Mysia on an island off the south coast of the Propontis connected to the mainland by a causeway or isthmus. The Roman poet Propertius calls it 'cool' and certainly the city has a well-ventilated position on the strait.[22] Hadrian visited Cyzicus in 123, and, according to the sixth-century author Johannes Malalas, found that the city had suffered a disastrous earthquake.[23]

Here he paved a market place with marble and founded a temple, described by Malalas as 'very large, one of the wonders' and by Dio as 'the biggest and most beautiful of all temples', though he does observe that 'in general the detail is more to be wondered at than praised'.[24] Hadrian's temple received possibly more than its fair share of plaudits when, in 166 or 167, the orator Aelius Aristides delivered a panegyric in Cyzicus, seizing on the temple as one of his main themes.[25] It competes with mountains; it is so great a landmark that navigators sailing to Cyzicus will no longer need beacon fires to guide them. Each of its blocks is as big as a temple, the temple itself as big as a sanctuary precinct, and the sanctuary precinct as big as a city. It is difficult to say whether there may be more marble in the temple than had been left over in its quarry on Prokonnesos. An anonymous poem in the *Greek Anthology* is in tune with this rodomontade, putting the building up there with the wonders of the world such as the pyramids and the colossus of Rhodes.[26] In view of this resonant hyperbole, there is something decidedly Ozymandias-like about the fate of this mighty structure. In the reign of Antoninus Pius, another earthquake struck Cyzicus and threw down the temple. Building this vast structure in a proven earthquake zone evinces rather more ambition than common sense. We may remember that Hadrian's additions to his family's home town of Italica in Spain likewise suffered collapse because it had been built on unstable clay. As poets have long noted, erecting buildings is not an infallible route to immortality.

Finally, we turn our attention to Cyrene, the foremost city in Cyrenaica in Africa. A Jewish revolt had broken out in this province in 115 in Trajan's reign and the resulting bloodbath had been accompanied by the targeting and destruction of many buildings associated with Roman rule and with Graeco-Roman culture and religion.[27] Inscriptions in Cyrene salute Hadrian as 'founder' and 'saviour' of the new city that rose phoenix-like out of the devastation. He built the 19-kilometre road connecting Cyrene to its port Apollonia. He rebuilt a bath complex with its porticoes and a ball-court. Another building he rebuilt, of a specifically Roman kind, was the temple of the Roman goddess Hecate. He later restored the Caesareum, a centre for the imperial cult, and went on to rebuild the judicial basilica where the Roman proconsul would administer justice. His final gift to the city, at the end of his reign, was a consignment of statues.[28]

In line with the hopes inherent in Hadrian's policy, the local elite were inspired to restore the temple of Isis and Artemis: Cyrene had been founded by Greeks from Thera and the rebuilding programme incorporated many Greek elements in acknowledgment of the city's heritage. But, as can be clearly seen in the list of his projects above, Rome was incorporated too and many of the buildings displayed Roman architectural characteristics. As Mary Boatwright observes, Cyrene's Roman present was acknowledged as well as its Greek past.[29]

Figure 17   Hadrian in Greek dress. © Trustees of the British Museum

Boatwright goes on to note that 'Hadrian's interest in Cyrene's Greek heritage seems reflected in the remarkable standing portrait of Hadrian installed in the city within a generation of his death (representing him in Greek dress, wearing a chiton and a himation [tunic and cloak])'. As Opper remarks, 'the statue – the only one of its kind – has become an iconic symbol of Hadrian, his politics and personality, and is illustrated to this day in every major book on his reign, if not in Roman art in general'.[30] Here stands the arch-philhellene. Except that, as Opper established in his great British Museum exhibition of 2008, he doesn't. When the statue was found in the ruins of the temple of Apollo in 1861, its component parts lay in different places: the body was broken in two and the hands and head were separate.[31] In fact, the head does not belong to the body. To make them fit, the Victorian restorers hid the join under thick layers of plaster. Opper concludes that 'as this statue can be physically exploded, so too can much of the popular myth of Hadrian as a peaceful Hellene'. Well, perhaps. Certainly, however, his love of Greek culture cannot be doubted and we shall explore this in the next chapter.

An exchange of poems

Hadrian's response to a grammarian's appeal shows that he was not always the friend of culture! A poem by a half-starved grammarian to the emperor Hadrian:

> One half of me is dead, the other starves:
> Save one, your majesty, of my two halves.

Hadrian's reply:

> With you the Sun and Pluto are annoyed:
> You look on one; the other you avoid.[32]

9

Hadrian and Athens

In 124 AD, Hadrian visited Athens for the first time as emperor. The *Graeculus* was to spend a year in the city and Greece as a whole. Athens was a somnolent university town and a sightseer's paradise, its great public buildings serving as vivid reminders of the city's period of greatness five centuries before. This chapter will outline the ways in which Hadrian sought to revivify its glory days.

Chameleon-like but with deep sincerity, Hadrian assimilated himself to the culture of Athens. He acted as a president of the Dionysia theatre festival in 125.[1] Dio tells us that 'he wore the local costume for the occasion and performed his role brilliantly'.[2] Even more significantly, it was almost certainly on this visit that Hadrian was initiated into the Eleusinian Mysteries.[3] These were centred at Eleusis, a city linked to Athens by the 22-kilometre Sacred Way. They were open to all adult speakers of Greek – men, women and slaves – and, in their ritual recreation of the earth goddess Demeter's descent to the underworld to rescue her daughter Kore (or Persephone), promised rebirth into immortal life. In the second and third centuries AD these mysteries were the most venerated of traditional Greek cults; they were viewed as Athens' gift to the Greek world at large.

The initiation ceremonies lasted a week. The young men who went to collect the sacred objects were by tradition armed, but the demands of security for the emperor meant that in 124 the custom was dropped.[4] Presumably, the other rituals proceeded as normal: an assembly which murderers and barbarians could not attend, a ritual bath in the sea with sacrifices to Demeter and Kore, and the great procession along the Sacred Way to Eleusis of more or less the whole population of Athens wearing saffron ribbons and myrtle crowns. Hadrian had a bridge built over the river Cephisus at Eleusis which would facilitate the journey along the Sacred Way.[5]

Five years later, in September 128, Hadrian participated in the mysteries once more.[6] Again there was the ritual bath in the sea, three days of fasting and the procession from Athens, this time going over Hadrian's new bridge. In the great chamber of initiation at Eleusis, he would have waited all night for the climactic moment when a great fire was lit and the priest cried out, 'The Mistress has borne a sacred child!' and showed the initiates the great mystery, an ear of corn cut in silence.[7] Only Augustus among the emperors had been through these rituals before Hadrian. Both of them may well have believed that they had been reborn to a new life.

During his stay in Athens from 124 to 125, Hadrian launched a massive building programme. The temple of Olympian Zeus had been planned on a vast scale and begun but then abandoned by the Athenian tyrant Peisistratus in the sixth century BC. Four hundred years later, King Antiochus IV Epiphanes of Syria had commissioned the Roman architect Cossutius to continue the work, but, on the king's death in 164 BC, the project was abandoned again. Then, in the early first century BC, the Roman general Sulla took some of the interior columns to Rome where they were used – appropriately enough – in the damaged temple of Jupiter, the Roman Zeus, on the Capitoline Hill. Now Hadrian finished the temple, adorning it with a vast statue of gold and ivory, following the example of the great sculptor Pheidias who had created his Zeus for Olympia and Athena for Athens from the same materials. The temple was finished with extraordinary speed. It was dedicated in the presence of the emperor in 131 or 132 AD, with his friend and travelling companion Polemon, the most famous Greek orator of the day, delivering a celebratory

Figure 18   The Temple of Olympian Zeus at Athens

address. The completion of this hugely ambitious project no doubt greatly enhanced Hadrian's prestige among his Greek subjects.

Other important public works in Athens included a new aqueduct bringing water to the city, a complex and challenging construction which took fifteen years to complete; a temple for Hera and Zeus Panhellenios; a Pantheon; and a new library with a hundred columns of Parian marble at the Roman city centre. Hadrian's friend Herodes Atticus donated a number of important buildings too. The area of Athens around the temple of Olympian Zeus was recognized as a new *deme* (a subdivision of the population), called Hadrianus (Hadrian's). The grand entrance gate, which still stands amid the traffic fumes of one of the busiest streets in the city, declares on the side facing the Acropolis, 'This is Athens, the ancient city of Theseus', the great mythical king of the city.[8] On the side facing the new city is the proud inscription, 'This is the city of Hadrian and not of Theseus'. With these two sentences, Hadrian was in fact following the example of Theseus who was said to have set up a column on the Isthmus

Figure 19   Hadrian's gate at Athens

of Corinth marking off the Peloponnese from Athenian territory in identical style. And the Roman emperor's two declarations are in iambic trimeters, the basic rhythm of Greek drama, just as the Athenian king's had been. The gate spoke to all who saw it just as the actors were doing in the theatre of Dionysus around the corner.

The outstanding example of Hadrian's commitment to and promotion of Greek culture was his creation in 131 to 132 of a Panhellenion, a commonwealth of Greek states with its centre at Athens. Dio Cassius tells us that 'he permitted the Greeks to build in his honour the shrine which was called the Panhellenion',[9] and some scholars have thought that Dio's phrasing means that the Panhellenion was a Greek initiative, not Hadrian's; but a badly-damaged decree from the Lydian city of Thyatira, set up in Athens to commemorate the city's admission to the body some time between 131 and 138, makes it evident that Hadrian was the moving spirit.[10] Part of it reads:

> [It was decided] to engrave this decree on a stone pillar and to set it up on the Acropolis so that it may be totally clear to all the Greeks how many things the city has obtained from the greatest king [Hadrian] inasmuch as both individually and publicly the king has bestowed benefits on all the Greek world, assembling from them that council, as a common mark of esteem, in the most brilliant city of the Athenians, the Benefactress, which grants to all at the same place the fruit of the [Eleusinian] Mysteries: the most revered Panhellenion ...

Hadrian was in fact replicating an initiative of the great Athenian statesman Pericles who, as Plutarch tells us, in the middle of the fifth century BC persuaded the Athenians to pass a decree:

> to invite all Greeks, wherever they lived in Europe and Asia and whether their cities were great or small, to send councillors to a conference at Athens to deliberate about the Greek sanctuaries which the barbarians had burned down [in the Persian invasion of Greece in 480 to 479 BC], the sacrifices which were owed to the gods in the name of Hellas [Greece] as a result of vows made when they were fighting the barbarians, and the security of the sea, in order that all might sail in it without fear and keep the peace.[11]

Pericles' proposal, coming from an increasingly imperialist Athens and inspired by a man who, according to Thucydides, saw his city as 'an education to Greece' (see the box at the end of this chapter), was clearly propagandist and was unsurprisingly spiked by the Spartans who were worried by their main rivals' increasing power.[12]

The Thyatira decree's unequivocal linking of the Panhellenion with admission to the Eleusinian Mysteries may look back to another initiative of the Athenians, missed by Hadrian scholars, from later in the fifth century BC, when they greatly expanded the festival at Eleusis by requiring their allies and inviting others to contribute a percentage of their agricultural produce to the goddesses Demeter and Kore. The Athenians were aiming to enhance the Panhellenic nature of the festival, looking back to a story told in the *Suda* (a tenth-century lexicon): 'Some say that famine took hold of all the land and the god said that the Athenians should perform a sacrifice, the *Proerosia*, to Demeter on behalf of all; on account of which they sent first-fruits to Athens from all parts as thank-offerings.'[13]

Whatever the outcome of the initiatives in the fifth century BC, the Panhellenion was a sensational success. Cities queued up to join, in a number of cases adding a spurious lustre to their suspect Greek credentials in order to do so. The show was very decidedly up and running when the Panhellenia games were celebrated for the first time in the summer of 137 AD. They were the centrepiece of the meetings, which were to take place every four years. The institution's influence went far beyond the networking city-states. As Doukellis observes, it 'functioned as a model of values and practices, which would subsequently guide the political and cultural choices of cities [in the eastern provinces] that were not members'.[14]

Modern interpretations of the Panhellenion have justly emphasized its importance as a centre of imperial cult. As Spawforth remarks, this emerges with particular clarity from the new findings that the Panhellenes wore crowns with imperial busts attached to them just like the provincial priests of the emperor.[15] Hadrian assumed the title of 'Panhellenius' in 132 AD and it was under this title that the living emperor was worshipped. Indeed, it may be for this reason that Dio tells us that the Panhellenion was a Greek initiative. While Asians were fully accepting of emperor-worship, mainland Greeks did not necessarily want to have it made too clear that Hadrian himself had created an institution in which he would be viewed as a deity. Compare and contrast Vespasian who had at least left it to his death throes before saying jocularly, during the onslaught of diarrhoea that finished him off, 'Oh dear, I think I am becoming a god.'[16]

Some interesting questions about the Panhellenion remain unanswered to this day. We do not even know where the headquarters of this considerable institution were located. It may be that meetings took place in the newly completed temple of Olympian Zeus. Another

---

A vision of Athens

The historian Thucydides, writing about Athens in her glory days in the fifth century BC, put the following words into the mouth of Pericles as part of his great funeral speech of 431 or 430 BC over those who had died in the first year of the Peloponnesian War:

In summary, I declare that our city as a whole is an education to Greece, and in each individual among us I see combined the personal self-sufficiency to enjoy the widest range of experience and the ability to adapt with consummate grace and ease. That this is no passing puff but factual reality is proved by the very power of the city: this character of ours built that power. Athens alone among contemporary states surpasses her reputation when brought to the test. Athens alone gives the enemies who meet her no cause for chagrin at being worsted by such opponents, and the subjects of her empire no cause to complain of undeserving rulers. Our power most certainly does not lack for witness: the proof is far and wide, and will make us the wonder of present and future generations. We have no need of a Homer to sing our praises, or of any encomiast whose poetic version may have immediate appeal but then fall foul of the actual truth. The fact is that we have forced every sea and every land to be open to our enterprise, and everywhere we have established permanent memorials of both failure and success.

This then is the city for which these men fought and died. They were nobly determined that she should not be lost: and all of us who survive should be willing to suffer for her.[19]

Figure 20   Pericles (Altes Museum, Berlin)

point is that we have no evidence as to whether Hadrian's wife Sabina accompanied him to its meetings. That she was in Greece for the 124 AD visit may be suggested by the fact that she was honoured as a 'New Demeter' at Megara when Hadrian went to that city.[17] Alternatively, or in addition, after Hadrian had begun his relationship with Antinous, did he appear with the beautiful youth at the Panhellenion as an exemplar of Greek love? One thing, however, remains certain. Even though the Cyrene statue of Hadrian as a pacific philhellene has been decisively exploded, it is scarcely misleading in the image of the emperor that it projects. At the same time, as Opper rightly insists, it must not be allowed to overshadow Hadrian's studied self-presentation as a martial figure. As we have seen, he did not follow in Alexander the Great's – or indeed Trajan's – wildly expansionist footsteps, but when his horse Borysthenes died in 122 AD, he aped the Macedonian's grief at the death of his steed Bucephalus, penning some admittedly undistinguished verses.[18] His carefully cultivated image as a formidable military force was to find horrific expression in his war with the Jews. But here in Greece, he was the irenic Hellenist, the propagator of all that was most civilized in Greek culture and revered in Greek religion. The Athenian Pericles had in fact been a general and was always portrayed in sculpture wearing a helmet – and not just because he wanted to conceal his large cranium! He was a hardy campaigner. The Athenian Hadrian, on the other hand, reinvented himself as the complete man of peace.

Antinous

In the splendidly refurbished Altes Museum on Berlin's Museum Island, the curators, in a stroke of delicious malice, have placed a bust of Hadrian between a bust of his wife Sabina and a statue of the boy Antinous, the love of his life. Sabina, we have already noted, may have claimed that, in order to protect the human race, she had ensured that she would not conceive a child by Hadrian.[1] We have reported too that Hadrian is said to have found her moody and shrewish[2] and to have broken up her familiar coterie when they were in Britain. The *HA* and the other sources for such statements are notoriously unreliable and we should probably

Figure 21   Sabina (Altes Museum, Berlin)

regard them with considerable suspicion. The assertions that Hadrian drove Sabina to suicide and that the rumour arose that he had poisoned her should doubtless be viewed in a similarly sceptical light.[3] However, the accumulation of such reports does give some support to the widely held belief that the marriage was far from happy.

Nevertheless, Hadrian's public manifestations of his attitude towards Sabina tell a very different story. He gave her the prestige of the title of Augusta as early as 119 AD, and in the funeral oration for her mother Matilda he referred to her as 'my Sabina'. Coins honouring her were regularly issued, their legends drawing attention to her virtues (such as piety and modesty) and the harmony between her and her husband (*concordia augusta*).[4] Statues in her honour were erected throughout the empire, usually together with images of Hadrian. In a much-restored relief commemorating her deification after her death, he looks on as she is carried aloft (Figure 22).[5]

From all of this, Sabina emerges as a decidedly opaque figure. Inscriptions tell us that she had a house in Rome as well as owning brickyards outside the city.[6] Opper justly observes that her changing portrait types show the alteration in fashions and hairstyles, which would of course have been imitated by women throughout the empire.[7] (The development of ladies' elaborate coiffeur over this period allows scholars to date female statues with some reliability.) On a more personal note, we know that, when she was in Egypt with her husband on the ill-fated expedition on which Antinous died, she and her companions went, after that event, to see the colossal statue of Memnon in Upper Egypt. Still a major tourist attraction, it is the northern twin of a pair of seated statues of the pharaoh. After it had been damaged in an earthquake, it emitted in the early mornings a weird oracular sound. One of Sabina's retinue called Balbilla carved four long poems – still legible – recording the party's presence, in the ancient Greek Aeolic dialect used by the famous poetess Sappho.[8] She referred to Hadrian as 'beloved by all the gods' and his 'lovely queen Sabina'. There is not a hint

Figure 22 Sabina's Apotheosis (Capitoline Museums, Rome). © Free Image Finder, 2013

of Antinous' demise. Ewen Bowie remarks – perhaps mischievously – that the way Balbilla refers to Sabina, combined with her imitation of the famous, in both senses Lesbian poetess, 'raises the question whether there was in fact a lesbian relationship between the two women, whether Balbilla was Sabina's answer to Hadrian's Antinous'.[9]

If we know little of Sabina, we have even less information about Antinous. We are not even sure whether he was a slave or free. He was a Greek from the city of Bithynion-Claudiopolis in western Asia Minor (Bolu in modern Turkey). Hadrian and he may have met when Antinous was a youthful teenager when the emperor toured the area in 123 AD, by now in his mid forties. If so, their relationship would have lasted for several years. Hadrian will doubtless have been attracted by Antinous' lushly sensual features. They may in addition have had a shared interest in hunting. A poem written after Antinous' death celebrates his prowess in a lion hunt in 130[10] and, as we know, Hadrian was obsessively keen on the sport, even writing epigrams on the qualities of his hunting dogs for the tombstones he set up where they fell.[11] A new city in Asia Minor was given the telling name Hadrianoutherai, 'Hadrian's Hunts'.

In the absence of anything else to record, we move on to Antinous' death. In the summer of 130 AD, Hadrian and his entourage, which included the Bithynian and Sabina, arrived in Egypt for an extended stay. In the autumn, they travelled up the Nile, reaching the city of Hermopolis. On 22 October, the Egyptians celebrated the traditional festival of the Nile and, two days later, they commemorated the death, by drowning in the river, and subsequent rebirth of the Egyptian god Osiris. It may have been on that very day that Antinous drowned.[12]

A question mark still hangs over his death. Dio, himself a Bithynian, reports that Antinous, who 'had become Hadrian's boy favourite', 'had died in Egypt, either after falling into the Nile, as Hadrian writes [in his lost autobiography] or, as the truth is, by being offered as a sacrifice. For ... Hadrian was very keen on the curious arts and employed divinations and incantations of all kinds.'[13] What Dio is suggesting here is that Hadrian, induced by bizarre superstitious beliefs, either persuaded or forced Antinous to take his life in order to prolong his own. It has also been proposed that Antinous committed suicide in despair at the fact that his increasing maturity would lose him the love of the boy-loving emperor. If the *HA* is correct in its assertion that Hadrian loved adult males, this is scarcely plausible.[14]

The death left the emperor shattered with grief, but, before we discuss his emotional reaction and its consequences, we should perhaps explore how the Romans would have regarded same-sex relationships of this kind. Discussion of homosexuality in the Greek and Roman worlds have been bedevilled, as James Davidson remarks of the former, by the tendency to limit discussion to who performed what genital action upon whom. With a relentless inevitability, sodomy becomes the main focus. It is hard to convey, writes Davidson, 'the pervasiveness of anal sex in the world of classicists today, most of them happily married men whose knowledge of sodomy tends to be the kind you get from books or dim rememberings of reckless nights at boarding school'.[15] Even if what Opper says is basically true, he falls into the trap of seeming to regard male same-sex love as a kind of business contract:

> In his sexual relationships the Roman male was expected to prove his dominance and virility. This, however, depended not on his choice of partner but on his role in intercourse. What mattered was to be the active partner, not the passive, penetrated.[16]

Craig Williams in his book *Roman Homosexuality* adds this valuable caveat:

> What was at stake was less a man's actual behaviour and more the *appearance* he gave and the *image* he had; how he was seen and talked about by his peers more than what he actually did in the privacy of his bedroom …[17]

By this criterion, what Hadrian and Antinous actually got up to behind closed doors is irrelevant. The former's masculine image appears to have remained intact throughout their relationship.

Things might not have proved so simple had Antinous been Roman rather than Greek, for free-born Roman boys seem to have been off-limits in such relationships. Indeed, Hadrian ran into criticism, if the *HA* is correct, for his love of mature males (already noted) and married women.[18] Williams argues that, in order to constitute a logical balance with the married women, who will have been Roman matrons, the males referred to here must be free Romans.[19] If the odium these liaisons attracted was due to the fact that they were regarded as out of bounds, clearly such sensitivities were in no way threatened by Hadrian's affair with a lovely Bithynian Greek, especially in a culture in which youthful male beauty was a more than acceptable topic to celebrate.[20]

No doubt the fact that he was emperor gave Hadrian increased licence. Opper points out that of the twelve rulers included in Suetonius' biographies of the Caesars, only two lack any homosexual proclivities.[21] Christian writers wrote with horror of Hadrian's relationship with 'this shameless and scandalous boy'[22] but otherwise, as Williams remarks,

> the relationship does not seem to have given rise to the kind of stinging gossip that we see directed against other emperors' sexual proclivities: for oral sex, for example, or for playing the receptive role in anal intercourse; for a scandalous desire for well-endowed men; for marrying a niece; for incestuous relations with a sister or a mother. No emperor was ever maligned for taking a beautiful young foreigner as a concubine.[23]

In such a relationship, there could be no doubt about who was the dominant partner.

In addition, a certain glamour was lent to the Hadrian/Antinous relationship by its parallelism with that between Jupiter, the king of the gods, and the Trojan boy prince Ganymede whom, in the guise of an eagle, he had snatched up to Mount Olympus to serve as his cup-bearer. James I of England invoked a similar religious parallel when justifying his relationship with George, Earl of Buckingham: 'I wish to speak in my own behalf,' he breathtakingly remarked, 'and not to have it thought to be a defect, for Jesus Christ did the same, and therefore I cannot be blamed. Christ had his John, and I have my George.' Jupiter's celebrated sexual appetite surely makes him a decidedly more apt point of reference than Jesus.

A further point is that an aura of homosexuality had pervaded Trajan's court. Dio Cassius, a source favourable to him, tells us of his passion for a male dancer called Pylades.[24] Hadrian, as we have seen, had entered into this spirit on two occasions by getting too close to his predecessor's cherished pages. According to the *HA*, 'he gave way to excess in his sensual pleasures', composing love poems about his favourite boys.[25] Hadrian's great Athenian friend Herodes Atticus installed his own version of Antinous in his household. On display in the same room in the Berlin Museum as the genuine article, this boy is decidedly inferior in beauty, perhaps evincing Herodes' tact. Despite his predilections, Trajan had successfully

Figure 23   Polydeuces, Herodes Atticus' boy favourite (Altes Museum, Berlin)

presented himself as a model family man.[26] Hadrian's outward show of devotion to Sabina may have accomplished something of the same purpose, but there can be scant doubt that his heart lay with Antinous. Nonetheless, despite such assertions as Opper's that 'a deep physical and emotional bond' must have developed between the two of them,[27] we have no evidence at all as to how the recipient of all that love felt about it.

A beautiful boy

Statius, a poet of the generation before Hadrian's, wrote a poem on the death of Glaucias, the boy favourite of one Atedius Melior. Here is an excerpt:

For a long time now, o rightly beloved boy, I have turned between choices as I seek for a worthy approach to embark on your praises. On one side your youthfulness, standing on the threshold of life, grabs my attention, on another your beauty, on another your precocious modesty, your sense of honour and your integrity, riper than your tender age. O, where are your fair complexion suffused with red blood and those starry eyes shining from heaven and the compact modesty of your small brow and your naturally flowing locks above with their soft fringe of lovely hair? Where, I wonder, is your talkative mouth with its charming complaints, your lips with their scent of spring flowers as you, Atedius, embraced him, your tears mingled with laughter, your voice, all its tones sweetened by Hybla's honeycombs, which would cause a snake to cease its hissing and cruel stepmothers to want to be your slave? What I say about his charms is all true. I am making nothing up. Alas the milk-white neck, the arms ever weighing upon his master's neck. O, where is the imminent hope of coming manhood, the longed-for adornment on his cheeks, the beard you often swore by? A grim hour, a hostile day has brought all to ashes. All that is left to us is to remember.[28]

Figure 24 Antinous as Osiris (Vatican Museums, Rome). © Stefano Baldini/The Bridgeman Art Library

What attracted criticism of Hadrian was not in fact his love affair with the living Antinous, but his behaviour after his death. The *HA* tells us that 'he wept like a woman'.[29] Dio goes into more detail:

He honoured him by founding [on October 30, 130 AD] a city on the spot where he had suffered this fate [of drowning] and named it Antinoopolis after him. And he set up statues, or rather sacred images of him over practically the whole world. And finally he said that he had seen a star which he took as that of Antinous and he eagerly listened to the false tales of his retinue who said that the star had really come into being from the soul of Antinous and had then appeared for the first time. On account of these things he became the object of mockery. Another factor was that on the death of his sister Paulina he had not immediately paid her any honour.[30]

It was in fact Hadrian's creation and lavish – and unprecedented – propagation of an Antinous cult following his death that provoked widespread hostility, especially from Christians who reacted strongly against the new cult's promise of salvation and rebirth after death, understandably wishing to suppress this rival to their own religion. In a recent book, Sam Moorhead and David Stuttart have suggested that Antinous is in fact an invention of Hadrian, who 'encouraged' tales of how he had been 'the emperor's companion, how he had drowned in the Nile, how in death he had become immortal – a carefully constructed matrix in which Antinous could become all things to all people, designed to bind the Roman world together in one universal belief'.[31] I can see no reason to be sceptical about the living and breathing Antinous we have described, but it certainly makes sense to believe that Hadrian, as well as finding expression for his overwhelming grief, was eager to propagate a cult that would enable the Greeks to feel they had a real stake in a religion established by a Roman empire. Moorhead and Stuttard suggestively assert that Hadrian's obsession with Hellenism combined with his interest in the mystery religions of the east such as those at Eleusis and on the Nile to inspire 'his invention of a new god, Antinous, a chameleon creation promising rebirth, who combined features of Greek and Roman deities such as Hermes, Pan and Dionysus as well as the Egyptian god Osiris.'[32]

The cult soon spread throughout the Roman world, to Greece, Asia, Africa and even to Britain where a bronze bust of Antinous has been found at Littlecote Villa in Wiltshire.[33] The senatorial elite were far from behindhand in its propagation. A huge seated statue of the boy god, for example, has recently been found at a country villa of Herodes Atticus at Luku in the eastern Peloponnese.[34] A portrait statue of him was found in Spain at the villa of the local governor near Tarragona. The intellectuals also were not slow to climb on board. Polemon, a figure we have already met as the leading sophist and orator of his day, sponsored the issue by the Smyrna mint of coins bearing Antinous' image. Opper informs us that about one hundred marble images of the new deity are currently known to archaeologists. And the cult survived the emperor's death.

Yet it is probably appropriate to conclude this chapter by focusing on Hadrian's sorrow. This is underlined by discoveries at his villa at Tivoli to which he returned in 134 AD. At least ten marble images of Antinous have been uncovered there and Italian archaeologists have recently found along one of the main access roads to the villa a large structure which they believe to have been a sanctuary, perhaps a monumental tomb, of Antinous.[35] The emperor and his distinguished visitors will have had before their eyes and in their thoughts the lovely face with its intense gaze and the powerful body of Hadrian's toy boy who had been translated into a god.

11

Christians and Jews

As we saw in the previous chapter, the polytheistic religions of Greece and Rome found it unproblematic to absorb new elements. Their lack of fundamentalism in fact made the Romans extremely tolerant of other religions, frequently assimilating them to their own. This does not necessarily mean that they were cynical about their cults, though some of them were. There was old-fashioned piety aplenty. A story told in Cicero's *Concerning the Nature of the Gods* well illustrates the folly of rejecting divine communication. In the First Punic War, the general Publius Claudius Pulcher consulted the sacred chickens about whether to fight a sea-battle with the Carthaginians. When the chickens refused to eat, he ordered them to be thrown into the sea so that, as he said in jocular contempt, 'they might drink since they refused to eat'.[1] He went ahead and fought the battle – which inevitably he lost.

One religion, however, totally resisted any absorption into the Roman system of beliefs. This was Christianity. The Gospel of Luke and the Acts of the Apostles make it clear that both Jesus and St Paul, the founder and propagator of the religion, were at home in the Roman world and did nothing against Rome's interests;[2] however, when committed Christians were forced to come clean about their beliefs, they simply refused to accept gods other than their own. We are all too aware of the challenges set by such fundamentalism in the modern world. Christians were far from popular. Suetonius refers to them as 'a breed of men of a new and noxious superstition'.[3] The historian Tacitus, another contemporary of Hadrian's, refers to their religion as 'a deadly superstition' and talks of 'their hatred of the human race.'[4] He tells how it took Nero's savagery to evoke the people's sympathy towards them when he scapegoated them for the great fire in Rome in 64 AD, dressing them in the hides of wild animals and having them torn to pieces by dogs, and burning them to serve as human torches in his garden by night.

A markedly more thoughtful approach to the Christians can be seen in the correspondence between Tacitus' friend Pliny and the emperor Trajan when the former was serving as governor of Bithynia from 109 or 110 AD. The exchange is the first pagan evidence of the Roman attitude to Christianity. (Tacitus' account of the fire in Rome was written later.) Pliny informs Trajan that he has interrogated those who have been denounced to him as Christians. If they persisted in their belief, he had them executed, feeling that, whatever the nature of their creed, 'their stubborn defiance and inflexible obstinacy' deserved punishment. He discharged those who said they were not Christians, if they invoked the Roman gods, offered adoration with wine and frankincense to Trajan's image and cursed Christ. Former Christians too were discharged if they went through the same procedure. Pliny concedes that at their meetings the Christians simply sing hymns and commit themselves to virtuous behaviour, but he still thinks of their religion as 'a contagious superstition'. In his characteristically courteous but efficient reply, Trajan expresses his approval of what Pliny has done, but says, in an enlightened spirit, that information laid by anonymous accusers must not be followed up.[5]

As for Hadrian's attitude to the Christians, we have at third-hand a letter he wrote to Licinius Silvanus Granianus, the proconsul of Asia, whose provincial council wanted him to take steps against them. The emperor says that Christians must be proved guilty of specific crimes before they can be sentenced. Thus 'the name alone' was insufficient to ensure conviction.[6] In addition, false accusation was to be severely punished. Hadrian was treading carefully. The last thing he wanted was a purge. Indeed, the Christian church historian Eusebius asserts that two Christians, Quadratus and an Athenian called Aristides, delivered a defence of their faith to the emperor.[7] If this is indeed the case, we know nothing of Hadrian's reaction.

Under Constantine (late third and early fourth century AD), Christianity was, of course, to gain the endorsement that led to its becoming the leading religion of the Roman empire. The history of Rome's dealings with the Jews and Judaism is, in contrast, deeply tragic. In his important book, *Rome and Jerusalem, The Clash of Ancient Civilizations*, Martin Goodman has shown how, in the early empire, relations between Romans and Jews were generally unproblematic. The latter were viewed by the former as strange, even exotic, but not as dangerous or hostile. Judaism in fact blossomed when Herod the Great dismantled and started to rebuild the Temple, Jerusalem's main institution and the epicentre of the religion. Work began in 20 or 19 BC and continued for decades. The result was a building of extraordinary magnificence, and pilgrims flocked to it.

The disastrous history of 66 to 70 AD which changed everything was, Goodman suggests, the result of a number of factors. A series of incompetent and venal governors of Judaea culminating in the astonishingly confrontational Gessius Florus led to a Jewish rebellion. The governor of Syria failed in his attempt to restore order, losing a huge number of men in the process. Rome would inevitably retaliate strongly. Vespasian, a Roman general from an undistinguished family (his father had been a tax farmer), and his son Titus were sent to the province to sort things out. This could no doubt have been managed without the appalling brutality and devastation that actually ensued. It was Vespasian's bid to become emperor that led to the destruction of Jerusalem.

Nero's suicide in 68 AD had inaugurated the so-called Year of the Four Caesars during which, amid scenes of grim carnage among Roman citizens, the empire was tossed like a blood-stained ball from

Galba to Otho and from Otho to Vitellius. Vespasian too joined the ball game and left Judaea, transferring the command of the legions there to the highly efficient hands of Titus. He successfully wrested the throne from Vitellius, but, in view of his unimpressive family background, a major victory was vital to lend validity to the new regime. By his brutal capture of Jerusalem, Titus, as Goodman puts it, made a resounding statement that the new emperor 'was not a thuggish nonentity propelled to power by the slaughter of Roman citizens in civil conflict but a hero of the Roman state who had won victory in Judaea'.[8]

The most traumatic blow for the Jews was the fact that when Titus sacked their city in 70 AD, their Temple was destroyed: the despoliation of its sacred objects is still visible in a frieze on the triumphal Arch of Titus in the Roman Forum. The sources are divided on whether Titus intended this to happen,[9] but once it had, it was inevitable that it would be presented as deliberate policy, a major gesture in the suppression of the Jews and their religion, which was now deemed unworthy to exist. The Romans prevented the rebuilding of the Temple, which remains in ruins to this day. Furthermore, throughout the duration of the empire, the Jewish population was forced to send its annual half-shekel (or two drachmas) each for the upkeep of the Temple and the support of its rituals to the Temple of Capitoline Jupiter in Rome, which had burnt down in 69 AD, instead. In addition, the Tenth Legion was permanently garrisoned at Jerusalem, putting the city at the centre of a militarized zone.

The policy of extreme repression was continued by successive emperors, with a short outbreak of more generous treatment under Nerva, up to the time of Hadrian. It seems probable that Arrian was referring to the Jews when he wrote that 'Trajan was determined above all, if it were possible, to destroy the nation completely, but if not, at least to crush it and stop its presumptuous wickedness'.[10]

In view of all this, it is scarcely surprising that some half a century after the sack of Jerusalem in 70 AD, revolt broke out again in 132 AD. To the above litany of grievances were now added Hadrian's plans for rebuilding the city as an important Roman colony with a huge temple of Jupiter near the site of the destroyed Temple. This must have made the extinction of Jewish life from the city seem imminent. To add insult to injury, a regulation that banned circumcision came into existence, proving a significant threat to Jewish identity.

Anthony Birley suggests that the trigger for the uprising may have been an omen which Dio says gave forewarning of the desolation of almost the whole of Judaea. 'For the tomb of Solomon, which the Jews hold as an object of veneration, disintegrated of itself and collapsed, and many wolves and hyenas ran howling into their cities.'[11] What, the Jews may have felt, did they have to lose?

Simon Bar Kokhba, the leader of the rebellion, remains a venerated figure in the Jewish tradition to this day, a Boudicca-like icon of national defiance of imperial oppression. Harsh, uncompromising and far from reluctant to go against the religious authorities who usually refer to him as Bar Koziba, 'Son of the Lie'[12] – though he had the support of the great Jewish religious authority Rabbi Akiba – he was a potent and inspirational mastermind in the guerrilla warfare, taking the title 'Prince of Israel'. The name Bar Kokhba is clearly a *nom de guerre* meaning 'Son of the Star' and referring to Balaam's prophecy of the Messiah in the *Book of Numbers*, 'I see him, but not nigh. There shall come forth a star out of Jacob. And a sceptre shall rise out of Israel. And shall smite through the corners of Moab, and break down all the sons of tumult.'[13] According to Jewish sources, Rabbi Akiba paid a high price for his support: he was arrested and put to death by the Romans.[14] It is worth remarking, in view of the topic with which this chapter began, that, because the Christians refused to join the revolt, they were regarded as enemies by the rebels. Unsurprisingly, therefore, later Christian writers are uniformly hostile to Bar Kokhba and the rebellion.

Describing the beginning of the rebellion, Dio tells us that, when the Jews were called upon to manufacture weapons for Rome, they deliberately made them of poor quality so that the Romans would reject them and they could use them themselves.[15]

> And they did not dare to risk a pitched battle with the Romans but they occupied advantageous positions in the country and strengthened them with underground passages and wells so that they would have places to flee to whenever they were hard-pressed and could meet together unnoticed under the ground. They made openings in these subterranean passages from above so that they could allow for ventilation and light.[16]

Spectacular finds from the caves in which guerrillas and civilians took refuge from the Roman army give an impression of life in the province before peace was so horrifically disrupted. Opper's catalogue of his British Museum exhibition contains some fine illustrations of artefacts from the Cave of Letters (so called because letters from Bar Kokhba were discovered there): three house keys, which Opper movingly calls 'a potent and eternal symbol of refugees all over the world'; a leather sandal; mirrors; bowls and jugs, some of them luxury items suggesting the presence of wealthy occupants; a date-fibre basket; and a nasty-looking knife.[17] These poignant items ram home the truth that real people suffered and died in this horrific episode.

Dio tells us that at first the Romans 'took no account' of the Jewish rebellion.[19] However, they changed their tune rapidly when two legions and about a dozen auxiliary regiments commanded by the legate Tineius Rufus were comprehensively crushed. Publicius Marcellus, the governor of Syria, rushed in with the Third Legion and other units, but, when the Twenty-Second Legion arrived from Egypt to provide support, it appears instead to have been wiped out: at all events, the Twenty-Second Legion stops being mentioned on the Roman army lists.[20]

A Scottish chieftain speaks out against Roman imperialism

Tacitus puts these words into the mouth of the Caledonian Calgacus as he is about to fight Agricola at Mons Graupius in 83 AD.[18] The Romans will win.

Every time that I survey the causes of this war and the dire straits to which we have been reduced, I have great hopes that this day on which you have gathered in unity will prove the beginning of liberty for the whole of Britain; for all of you together here are as yet unmarked by slavery, and there is no land behind us and not even the sea is safe from the threat of the Roman fleet. And so the very battle and arms that bring honour to the brave are also the safest resort for cowards. Previous battles, which were fought against the Romans with varying outcomes, left behind them the hopes of help in our hands, seeing that we, the noblest spirits of the whole of Britain who for that reason dwell in its inmost shrine, had never seen any shores of the enslaved and had kept our very eyes unpolluted by contact with tyranny. The very remoteness of this land of rumour has protected us to this day where we dwell at the world's end on the final verge of freedom. Now the furthest bounds of Britain lie exposed and what is unknown is always thought to be magnificent [and is thus irresistible to the Romans]. But there are no other tribes behind us, nothing except waves and rocks and, still more deadly than these, the Romans whose arrogance it would be useless to try to escape by obedience and self-control. Rapists of the world, now that no land is left to suffer the devastation that they bring to everything, they are probing the sea. If their enemy is rich, they are greedy, if poor, glory is their goal. Neither the East nor the West will make them feel that they have won enough. They are the only nation in the world who covet wealth and want with equal passion. To plunder, butcher, steal – that's what they wrongly call empire. They make a desert and call it peace.

Such was the seriousness of the situation that Hadrian himself came to the province and it may be that he asked the architect Apollodorus, whose contretemps with the emperor we have discussed earlier, for advice about siege engines.[21] (Further evidence that the story in Dio of Hadrian's having him killed is a fiction.) Appalled by the scale of Roman losses, the emperor omitted the customary cheery opening from his letter to the senate: 'If you yourselves and your children are in health, that is splendid. I and the legions are in health.'[22]

The nature of the crisis led Hadrian to summon Sextus Julius Severus all the way from Britain where he was governor to take charge of operations in Judaea. Meanwhile, with considerably increased troop numbers, Tineius Rufus wreaked terrible revenge on the Jewish population. Eusebius tells us that 'when military aid had been sent him by the emperor, he moved out against the Jews, treating their madness without mercy. He destroyed in heaps thousands of men, women and children, and under the law of war, enslaved their land.'[23] On his arrival, possibly early in 134 AD, Severus pursued a policy of gradual extermination. According to Dio:

> he did not dare to attack the enemy in the open at any one point since he saw how many and how desperate they were. But by intercepting small groups because of the number of his soldiers and under-officers, and by depriving them of food and keeping them shut up, he was able, fairly slowly but at the same time comparatively easily, to crush them, wear them down and eliminate them. Very few of them in fact survived. 50 of their most significant guard posts and 85 of their most famous villages were razed to the ground. 580,000 men were slaughtered in the raids and battle, and it was impossible to discover the number of those killed by disease and fire.[24]

Dio adds laconically that 'many Romans also died in this war.'[25]

The Romans may not have achieved final victory until 136 AD. In the last year or the year before, Bar Kokhba was killed after a last stand at the fortress of Bethar. According to Eusebius, the siege 'lasted a long time before the rebels were driven to desperation by famine and thirst and the instigator of their madness paid the penalty he deserved'.[26] One account tells us that his head was taken to Hadrian,[27] though it is likely that he had left Judaea by then and that Severus was the recipient of the grisly present. The slave market was afterwards flooded with Jewish captives.

After the suppression of the revolt, the Roman juggernaut resumed business. Celebrations of victory were on a muted scale; there was very little of the triumphalism displayed after the sack of Jerusalem in 70 AD, to this day proudly evident on the Arch of Titus in the forum in Rome, the only surviving triumphal arch that actually portrays a triumph. However, the rebuilding of Jerusalem as the pagan city Aelia Capitolina from which Jews were banned was renewed and completed. A statue of Hadrian on horseback was built on the site of the Temple[28] together with an image of Jupiter. A marble image of a pig, probably in fact a wild boar, the emblem of the Tenth Legion, was set up outside the gate on the Bethlehem road.[29] The ban on circumcision remained, and the province was no longer to be called Judaea but Syria Palestina. It is no wonder that when Hadrian's name occurs in rabbinical literature, it is usually accompanied by the curse, 'May his bones rot!'[30]

This ghastly anticipation of the holocaust marks a tragic breakdown in what we have seen as Hadrian's military policy. The Greek travel writer Pausanias, a contemporary, wrote of Hadrian as a figure 'who was extremely pious in the honour he paid to divinity and contributed very much to the happiness of all whom he ruled. He never went to war willingly, though when the Hebrews beyond Syria revolted he subdued them.'[31] This genocidal process towards the end of Hadrian's life makes it impossible to ignore an uncompromisingly brutal aspect to his make-up. This is grimly in line with much else that characterizes his last years.

12

The End

Even if he is mistaken about affairs being settled in the East, Aurelius Victor presents a positive view of Hadrian on his return to Rome in 134 AD:

> More favourably disposed to eloquence and intellectual pursuits after creating peace in the east, Hadrian returned to Rome. Here, in the manner of the Greeks or of Pompilius Numa [the religious and peace-loving second king of Rome] he began to engage with religious ceremonies, the laws, the gymnasia, and teachers, to such an extent indeed that he even established a school for the liberal arts, which they call the Athenaeum, as well as devoting himself to the mysteries of Ceres [Demeter] and Libera [Korē], which are called the Eleusinian Mysteries, at Rome in the manner of the Athenians.[1]

He even made a belated gesture of reconciliation to his old enemy, his brother-in-law Servianus whom he allowed to serve as consul, for the third time, at the age of 84.[2] However, as we shall see, that hatchet was not to remain buried for long. And it may not be fanciful to take a story of Dio's about Hadrian's less-than-generous behaviour at the chariot races as an indication that the well-springs of good nature were drying up in him:

> After he had returned to Rome, the crowd at a spectacle shouted out their request that a certain charioteer should be freed. He gave his answer in writing on a notice-board: 'It is not right for you either to ask me to free another's slave or to force his master to do so.'[3]

Certainly Hadrian now began to turn against a number of long-standing friends.[4] Though he had known Platorius Nepos for perhaps

40 years and had even thought of him as a possible successor, his affection turned to hate.[5] Influenced by 'whatever was whispered about his friends', Hadrian came to regard Attianus and Septicius Clarus, Prefects from early in his reign, 'in the category of enemy'.[6] The *HA* bluntly tells us that 'he forced Polyaenus and Marcellus to commit suicide'.[7] Two close equestrian advisers, Valerius Eudaemon and Avidius Heliodorus, also fell into disfavour, the former being reduced to poverty,[8] though the latter appears to have been restored to favour by 137. It seems as if Hadrian wanted the extraordinarily committed Prefect of the Guard Marcius Turbo to retire.[9] Failing to take the hint, he was eventually removed.

Spying on his friends

An extract from the *Historia Augusta* (11.4–6):

> He kept a close eye not only on his own household but also on his friends. As a result he used his police agents to pry into all their secrets, yet his friends didn't realize that their private lives were known to the emperor until the emperor himself revealed this. In this connection it will be helpful to include an incident from which we can tell that he found out a great deal about his friends. Somebody's wife wrote to her husband complaining that his devotion to pleasures and bath houses was making him reluctant to come back home to her, and Hadrian found this out through his agents. And so, when the man sought leave of absence, Hadrian criticized him over the bath houses and pleasures. The man responded, 'What, did my wife write to you just what she wrote to me?' People consider this his worst fault …

From early in his reign, Hadrian had been planning a monumental tomb for himself and his successors. One model would inevitably be the great mausoleum of Augustus, the imposing structure on the

Campus Martius on the west bank of the Tiber, which had made it clear that the emperor, however emphatically he termed himself simply 'the first citizen', was in fact planning a dynastic succession. Here were stored the ashes of the Caesars. Vespasian, Titus and Domitian lay in a new monument on the Caelian Hill. Nerva, the stopgap emperor between Domitian and Trajan, had been interred in the Mausoleum of Augustus, after which it was sealed. Trajan's remains, and later those of his wife Plotina, were installed in the base of his column. Hadrian would be the first occupant of his new structure, which, the dates on the brick-stamps suggest, he began as early as 123 AD.

Built on the east bank of the Tiber outside the sacred border of the city, it attained, indeed still attains, total dominance of the surrounding area. A new monumental bridge, the Pons Aelius, decorated with impressive sculptures, led to it across the Tiber. The mausoleum was 50 metres high and was surrounded by a fence of metal grilles between travertine pillars, some 115 metres long on each side. Large peacocks of gilded bronze, symbols of eternal life, crowned the fence pillars. The central drum, inevitably made of concrete and faced with tufa and travertine blocks, had a diameter of 74 metres, reducing to 68 metres, and its total height was 31 metres. The burial chamber was in the top of the drum and this was surmounted by a tower which was in its turn crowned with a huge sculpture, presumably showing Hadrian being borne aloft in the heavens in a four-horse chariot.

We know nothing certain of the monument's superstructure, but architectural remains and the literary record suggest that it was lavishly decorated with sculptures.[10] In the sixth century AD, Procopius tells us that there were marble statues of men and horses on top of the mausoleum, many of which were hurled down on the besieging Goths in 537 AD. The twelfth-century *Mirabilia Urbis Romae* refers to gilded bronze horses at the corners of the monument and, in addition to the peacocks on the surrounding fence, a bronze

Figure 25   Hadrian's Mausoleum, now the Castel Sant'Angelo, and the Pons Aelius

bull. Opper's summation is instructive: 'In total, these remains suggest a monument more similar in the richness of its sculptural décor to the Mausoleum of Halicarnassus, one of the wonders of the ancient world, than the tomb of Augustus with its sombre, tree-lined earthen mound.'[11]

Today, the monument survives as a vast fort. It is crowned not by a monumental group portraying Hadrian on his way to join the gods, but by a magnificent bronze of St Michael, sword and spear in hand. The original sculptures have long disappeared from the bridge. They have been replaced by a parade of angels sculpted by Bernini, one of the great architects of papal Rome. Vast fortifications surround what we now know as the Castel Sant'Angelo. Opera-lovers recognize it as the castle from whose walls Tosca performs her celebrated leap. The whole complex is in fact a frequently overwritten palimpsest entirely characteristic of the eternal city. Yet the display of Hadrian's final poem – of which more anon – within the drum ensures that the innumerable visitors are reminded of the monument's original melancholy yet celebratory purpose.

In 136 AD, Dio records, Hadrian 'now began to be ill, for he had already been subject to nose-bleeds before this and at this time they became considerably worse'.[12] It was time for the childless emperor to think about the succession. In the second half of the year, he declared that he was adopting as his son one of the consuls, Lucius Ceionius Commodus. The *HA* declares, with possible malice, that Commodus' sole recommendation was his 'beauty'.[13] However, he is unlikely to have been a member of any imperial homosexual set since he was notorious for his pursuit of women.[14] (He is reported to have known Ovid's books of *Amores* (Love poems) by heart.)[15] Commodus was the stepson of one of the four senators who had been killed at the start of Hadrian's reign, but it is hard to believe that the emperor was at last making amends for something that had happened 18 years before. The choice of Commodus – or Lucius Aelius Caesar as he now became – is especially puzzling in view of the fact that he was tubercular, frequently coughing up blood, as Dio tells us.[16] Indeed, he was too ill to thank Hadrian in the senate for adopting him.[17] However, one of Aelius' daughters was engaged to the fifteen-year-old Marcus Annius Verus, a youthful member of Rome's Spanish mafia and a particular favourite of the emperor, who called him *Verissimus* (truest, sincerest).[18] Hadrian's intention may have been that the frail Aelius, now in his thirties, should keep the throne warm for Marcus until the latter grew up. Aelius was now sent on a military command to Pannonia, presumably to win favour with the army.

Whatever Hadrian's thinking was in his choice of Aelius, the *HA* tells us that 'everyone else was against it'.[19] He had passed over members of his family, understandably in the case of his newly recon-ciled but decidedly aged brother-in-law Servianus, but surprisingly

with regard to the youthful Pedanius Fuscus, grandson of Servianus
and his wife, Hadrian's sister Domitia Paulina. The *HA* informs us
that Pedanius' hope of becoming emperor was precisely the reason
for Hadrian's hatred. The sources do not tell us exactly what happened
next, but it appears that in 137 AD, Fuscus made some kind of move
against Hadrian and was executed, while Servianus was forced to
commit suicide, either then or later. Dio puts that matter somewhat
cryptically: 'Servianus and his grandson Fuscus ... were put to death
on the grounds that they were displeased' at the adoption of Aelius.[20]
Dio also gives us a memorable account of Servianus' last moments:
'He asked for fire, and, as he offered incense, cried out, "That I am
guilty of no wrong, you gods are well aware. As for Hadrian, this is
my only prayer: may he long for death but be unable to die".[21] The
gods appear to have hearkened to his prayer. The crowning irony
came when Aelius' health degenerated in Pannonia, forcing him to
return to Rome, and he died there the night before 1 January 138. At
about the same time, Hadrian's wife Sabina died too.

On 24 January 138, his sixty-second birthday,[22] Hadrian, 'by now
consumptive as a result of serious haemorrhaging, which had led to
dropsy, ... summoned the most prominent and respected senators
to his house', and from his sickbed, announced his new choice of
successor, praising the superiority of an adoptive over a natural son
who might be mentally defective or a cripple.[23] This was the 51-year-old
Titus Aurelius Boianius Arrius Antoninus, a rich aristocrat whose
family background lay in southern Gaul and who was one of Hadrian's
close advisers. Antoninus was adopted on 25 February and on the
same day was made to adopt Aelius' son Lucius Ceionius Commodus
as well as Marcus Annius Verus, Hadrian's favoured *Verissimus*. This
arrangement proved unpopular with some members of the senate,
but their voices were suppressed, apparently without violence.[24] Now
everybody knew where they stood and stability was assured. The
question mark which had hung over the succession to the previous

emperor had been replaced by clarity. Indeed, Hadrian's choices determined the next two emperors. Marcus was to become Antoninus' successor: we know him as Marcus Aurelius. Hadrian's success in establishing this continuity over two generations is remarkable.

His health was now deteriorating fast. Recourse to charms and magic rites proved of no lasting avail with his dropsy.[25] Dio tells us that 'as he was in fact continuously getting worse and could be said to have been dying day by day, he began to long for death. Often he asked for poison or a sword, but no one would give them to him.' Hadrian 'bitterly lamented that state to which his illness and his helplessness had brought him, in that he was not able to do away with himself despite the fact that it was still in his power, even when on the verge of death, to destroy anyone else.'[26]

On one occasion, by a mixture of threats and promises, Hadrian persuaded a huntsman called Mastor to strike him at a spot below his nipple which his doctor recommended and he had marked in colour. Mastor panicked and could not perform the task. The *HA* reports what happened then:

> Antoninus and the Prefects went in to Hadrian and begged him to endure the necessity of the disease with equanimity. Antoninus said that he would be a parricide if, after being adopted, he allowed him to be killed. Hadrian was angry at this and ordered the person who had informed them to be killed – he was, however, saved by Antoninus. He at once wrote his will. But he did not lay aside the business of the state. After making his will, he did indeed try to kill himself again; when the dagger was taken from him he became more violent. He asked his doctor for poison, but he killed himself rather than give it to him. [27]

Servianus' prayer was being fulfilled to the letter.

It was at a late stage of his life that Hadrian wrote his now-lost autobiography, which was available to Dio and the author of the *HA*.[28] It may be that it was written in the form of a letter to Antoninus, some of which survives.[29] In it Hadrian insists:

I want you to know that I am being released from life neither prematurely nor unreasonably; I am not full of self-pity nor am I surprised and my faculties are unimpaired – even though I may almost appear, as I have realized, to do injury to you when you are at my side, whenever I am in need of attendance, consoling me and encouraging me to rest. This is why I am impelled to write to you, not – by Zeus – as one who subtly devises a tedious account contrary to the truth, but rather making a simple and accurate record of the facts themselves.

We know that in his autobiography, Hadrian gave his self-exculpating account of the death of four consulars in 118, and insisted that Antinous had died by accidental drowning and for no other reason; and it may also have been in the autobiography that he asserted that Vespasian had been poisoned by his son and successor Titus, dubbed by Eutropius 'the beloved and darling of the human race'.[30]

Also at the end of his life, he composed a touchingly unpretentious poem about the journey his soul was about to take:

Little soul, little wanderer, little charmer,
guest and companion of the body,
where are you off to now?
to darkling, cold and gloomy places –
and you won't make your customary jokes.

The sense of humour to which Hadrian here lays claim has not been a notable feature of this account of his life.

The end came at his villa at Baiae on the bay of Naples on 10 July 138. Dio's account is dramatic: 'Finally he abandoned his careful regimen and by indulging in unsuitable food and drink met his end shouting aloud the popular saying: "Many doctors have killed a king!"'[31]

According to the *HA*, he died 'hated by all'.[32] (The Latin *inuisus* could also mean 'unseen' and refer to his death at distant Baiae, but Dio confirms the pejorative meaning.)[33] He was provisionally buried at the neighbouring port of Puteoli in the grounds of the former villa of Cicero, a celebrated figure from the dying days of the Roman republic. Such was the feeling against Hadrian among the senators that Antoninus, now emperor only four months after his adoption, had his work cut out to get them to decree that Hadrian should be deified. He eventually resorted to blackmail, claiming that if they failed to do so, his own adoption would be thrown into doubt. The senate capitulated, granting Hadrian divine honours and awarding Antoninus the title Pius (pious, reverent) in acknowledgement of his devotion to his adoptive father. Now at last Hadrian would make his final journey. He was cremated in effigy on a magnificent pyre in the Campus Martius; an eagle soared aloft from a hidden cage, its flight to the heavens symbolizing the emperor's apotheosis. And his remains were installed in the vast mausoleum he had built for himself.

His touchingly human final poem, however, suggests that he thought his soul might be bound not for the heavens but for the 'darkling, cold and gloomy places' of the underworld. His words nod unmistakably to Ennius – a poet whom, as we know, he preferred to the classic Virgil – and his description of the realms of the dead below the earth.[34] The contradiction between this private pessimism and the bright confident public show is reflected in the discordant balance of qualities that struck Hadrian's ancient biographers. The *HA* tells us that 'in one and the same person he was stern and kindly, serious and playful, hesitant and impetuous, mean and generous, hypocritical and straightforward, cruel and merciful, and always in all things changeable'.[35] His portraits have little sense of personality. Their marble or bronze curiously opaque, they reveal nothing about him, though the deep creases they show on both lower earlobes have suggested to medical experts that he may have been liable to coronary artery disease.[36] We shall probably search in vain for consistency in his character, though his cruelty, evinced above all in his genocide of the Jews, may well give us pause.

Birley remarks perceptively of Hadrian's poem that it seems

only fitting that the great traveller, who had so often accepted hospitality and who had taken a train of [companions] with him, should at the last have thought of his soul as a wanderer, ready to take off, this time for the underworld, his soul that had been his body's [host] and [companion].[37]

Figure 26   Hadrian. © Vatican Museum

And it is appropriate that we should take our leave of him in his most notable guise as a restless traveller.

Hadrian's journeys around the empire gave it an unprecedented cultural and religious coherence. His building programme renewed its fabric: Athens and Rome were but two of the vast number of cities that were totally transformed. His military policy of containment of the empire rather than its expansion ensured a welcome peace – even if the Jewish tragedy is a horrific instance of the words Tacitus puts into a British chieftain's mouth, 'the Romans make a desert and call it peace' (see Chapter 11). Aelius Aristides was wrong to comment that there was 'no need for him to wear himself out, travelling around the whole empire, no need for him now in one place now in another to check on every detail'.[38] Hadrian's presence everywhere and his total commitment to every undertaking were inspirational. He got things done. Notwithstanding his vices, his virtues enabled the *Graeculus* to refashion the Roman world of Augustus after his own ideals.

Notes

Introduction

1 The now-defunct shilling was a British coin of small value.
2 Rathbone (2008), 10–11.
3 Birley (1997), xiv.

Chapter 1

1 69.11.2–4.

Chapter 2

1 Tacitus, *Annals* 11.24.
2 *Geography* 3.2.15.
3 3.1.6.
4 3.2.14.
5 3.2.8.
6 Beard (2008), 21.
7 *Natural History* 31.87–8.
8 Opper (2008), 40.
9 Claridge (1998), 367–8; Opper (2008), 38–9.
10 Pliny, *Letters* 5.12; *HA Verus* 2.5; Gellius, *Noctes Atticae* 11.15.3.
11 *HA Hadrian* 16.6.
12 Bowie (1970), 3–41.
13 *HA Hadrian* 1.5.
14 Harlow and Laurence (2002), Chapter 5.
15 Suetonius, *Caligula* 10.1.
16 Davidson (2007), 81.

17 581a.13–17.

18 Harlow and Laurence (2002), 68.

19 *Laelius* 1.

20 Birley (1997), 23.

21 2.18.

22 Callistratus, *Digest* 48.19.28.3.

23 *HA Hadrian* 2.1–2.

24 *On Hunting* 12.1.

25 Bowie (1970), 26.

26 8.365–8.

27 Vout (2007), 59–60.

28 *HA Hadrian* 21.4.

29 Richardson (1996), 222.

30 *HA Hadrian* 2.2.

31 Fündling (2006).

32 Uden (forthcoming), Chapter 3.

33 Juvenal, *Satires* 3.58–61, 73–8.

Chapter 3

1 Tacitus, *Agricola* 41.2–42.5.

2 *Agricola* 45.2.

3 *Epigrams* 8 and 9; sense of decency: 9.79.6–8; Pitcher (1990), 86–8, cf. Tacitus, *Histories* 4.40.1.

4 *HA Hadrian* 2.2; *ILS* 308 in Smallwood (1966), 109.

5 *ILS* 308 in Smallwood (1966), 109.

6 *HA Hadrian* 2.2–3.

7 *HA Hadrian* 2.3.

8 Pliny the Younger, *Panegyricus* 6, 8.1–3; Dio Cassius 68.3.3–4; *Epit. de Caes.* 12.6–8.

9 *HA Hadrian* 2.5–6.

10 *HA Hadrian* 2.6.

11 *HA Hadrian* 2.6.

12 *HA Hadrian* 2.7.

13 Southern (2007), 146.

14 *HA Hadrian* 2.10.

15 *HA Hadrian* 2.10.

16 Birley (1997), 45.

17 *HA Hadrian* 3.2–3.

18 *HA Hadrian* 3.4.

19 *HA Hadrian* 3.8.

20 Dio Cassius 68.10.3.

21 *HA Hadrian* 3.6.

22 Roth (2009), 202.

23 *HA Hadrian* 3.6.

24 *ILS* 308 in Smallwood (1966), 109.

25 *HA Hadrian* 3.7.

26 Rossi (1971), 99, 130–212.

27 Claridge (1993).

28 Smallwood (1966) 328; Speidel (2006), 10.

29 69.9.2.

30 69.9.3–4.

31 Roth (2009), 202.

Chapter 4

1 *HA Hadrian* 3.9.

2 Zsidi (1994), 213.

3 *HA Hadrian* 3.10.

4 *HA Hadrian* 3.11.

5 Smallwood (1966), 445.

6 Opper (2008), 72.

7 James (2011), 189–90.

8 *HA Hadrian* 26.1.

9 *Anthologia Palatina* 6.332.

10 Dio Cassius 68.21.2–3.

11 Arrian, *Parthica* fr. 46.

12 *HA Hadrian* 4.4, 4.6.

13 *HA Hadrian* 4.10.

14 *HA Hadrian* 4.5.

15 *HA Hadrian* 7.2.

16 *HA Hadrian* 7.4.

17 *HA Hadrian* 7.6; Dio Cassius 69.8.1.

18 *HA Hadrian* 5.2.

19 Dio Cassius 68.32.2.

20 Fronto, *Principia Historiae* 11 (Van den Hout (1988), 209); Eutropius, *Breviarium* 8.6.2; *HA Hadrian*. 5.3, 9.1.

21 Dio Cassius 68.13.6.

22 For example, *Annals* 4.32.1–2.

23 *HA Hadrian* 5.1.

24 Tacitus *Annals* 1.11.

25 *Aeneid* 1.279.

26 Moorhead and Stuttard (2012), 129.

27 *HA Hadrian* 12.6. For an excellent account of Hadrian's barriers with first-class plans, maps and reconstructions, see Breeze (2011), Chapter 7.

28 Birley (1997), 116.

29 Opper (2008), 86.

30 *Agricola* 21.

31 *Epit. de Caes.* 14.8.

32 See also Godwin (1986), 12–13.

33 *HA Hadrian* 11.3.

34 *HA Hadrian* 11.3.

Chapter 5

1 Suetonius, *Iulius* 7.1, cf. Plutarch, *Caesar* 11.3.

2 *HA Hadrian* 10.2–5.

3 *RIC* III 246–7 (MS).

4 Suetonius, *Iulius* 49.

5 *HA Hadrian* 19.2; Fronto (Loeb 2, 206–7).

6 Opper (2008), 100–1.

7   53.27.2.

8   Wilson Jones (2000), 182–4.

9   Opper (2008), 120–1.

10 Opper (2008), 121–3.

11 Claridge (1998), 42, 45–7; Ling (1997).

12 Dio Cassius 69.7.1.

13 Opper (2008), 125.

14 Hannah and Magli (2011).

15 4.146.

16 *HA Hadrian* 19.12.

17 Boatwright (1987), 236.

Chapter 6

1   Opper (2008), 132–65.

2   Opper (2008), 240, n. 2.

3   *Epit. de Caes.* 14.5.

4   Opper (2008), 154.

5   *HA Hadrian* 26.5. There is no evidence at all as to which parts of the villa can be identified with these locations.

6   Spencer (2010), 174.

7   MacDonald and Pinto (1995), 81–94.

8   *Vita Apollonii* 8.20.

9   Dio Cassius 69.4.1–5.

10 For example, Ridley (1989).

11 Strabo, *Geography* 14.5.2.

12 Dio Cassius 54.23.2–4.

13 Jones and Sidwell (1997), 170.

14 Galen 5.17f. K.

15 Cato, *De Agricultura* 2.7.

16 Boatwright (2008), 169–71; *HA Hadrian* 18.7.

17 Seneca, *Letters* 47; see also Pliny, *Letters* 5.19, 8.16.

18 Apuleius, *Metamorphoses* 9.12 (trans. E. J. Kenney).

Chapter 7

1 *Satires* 10.80–1.

2 Goodman (2007), 51.

3 Danziger and Purcell (2005), 33–4.

4 *HA Hadrian* 19.10; Dio Cassius 69.8.2.

5 *HA Hadrian* 17.5.

6 Celsus, *On Medicine* 5.26, 28d, quoted in Beard (2008), 247.

7 Danziger and Purcell (2005), 34.

8 Goodman (2007), 43.

9 *Satires* 2.6.60.

10 *Letters* 56.1–2.

11 *HA Hadrian* 19.8.

12 *HA Hadrian* 19.2–3.

13 *Letters* 7.3–5.

14 *Childe Harold's Pilgrimage* 4.141.

15 *Confessions* 6.8.

16 Hopkins and Beard (2005), 118.

17 Hopkins and Beard (2005), 120.

18 Hopkins and Beard (2005), 98.

19 Cicero, *ad familiars* 7.1.3.

20 *Sunday Telegraph*, 15 April 2012, 25.

21 Hopkins and Beard (2005), 110–11.

22 *HA Hadrian* 3.8.

23 Martial, *De Spectaculis* 9.

24 *Letters* 9.6.

25 *Letters* 6.34.

26 Dio Cassius 69.7.1; 69.16.3.

27 Everitt (2010), 63–4; *CIL* 6 1000 48; *ILS* 5287.

28 Goodman (2007), 306; Ovid, *Ars Amatoria* 1.167; Martial, *Epigrams* 11.1.15; Juvenal, *Satires* 11.201–2; Tertullian, *De Spectaculis* 16; Balsdon (1969), 321.

Chapter 8

1 Birley (1997), xiv.

2 *HA Hadrian* 16.3–4; Birley (1997), 143 (translations are Birley's). The journeys are fleshed out in Speller (2002).

3 *HA Hadrian* 12.2–13.5.

4 Goodman (2007), 124, illustrations 13–16.

5 *HA Hadrian* 17.8.

6 *HA Hadrian* 17.9.

7 *Epit. de Caes.* 14.4.5.

8 Millar (1977), 33–5.

9 *IGRom.* III 1054.

10 Millar (1977), 33–5.

11 *Panegyricus* 20.3–4.

12 *HA Antoninus Pius* 7.11.

13 Mamertinus, *Panegyric* III (11).10.5 (trans. Millar).

14 Burrell (2004), 282.

15 Josephus, *Bellum Judaicum* 7.108–9.

16 Dio Cassius 69.6.3.

17 Philostratos, *Lives of the Sophists* 1.25.2 (531).

18 Smyrna inscription 4 lvS 697.

19 Philostratos, *Lives of the Sophists* 1.25.3 (532).

20 Birley (1997), 261.

21 Burrell (2004), 66–7.

22 Prop. 3.22.1. For the metapoetic overtones of the Latin word for 'cool', see Heyworth and Morwood (2011), 316.

23 Burrell (2004), 86–7; Malalas 11.16 ed. Dindorf (Bonn, 1831), 279; *Chronicon Pascale* 475.10 (Dindorf).

24 Dio Cassius 70.4.1–2.

25 Oration 27 Keith 125, 135.

26 9.656.

27 Dio Cassius 68.32.1–3.

28 *SEG* IX 136.

29 Boatwright (2000), 174, 177, 179, 180, 182.

30 Opper (2008), 69.

31 Opper (2008), 70.

32 *Greek Anthology* 9.137. Pluto was king of the underworld.

Chapter 9

1 *HA Hadrian* 13.1.

2 69.16.1.

3 *HA Hadrian* 13.1; Dio Cassius 69.11.1.

4 *HA Hadrian* 13.2.

5 Jerome, *Chronica* 198 Helm.

6 Inferred from *IG* II/III² 2040.

7 Clement of Alexandria, *Protrepticus* 2.12.

8 *IG* II² 5185.

9 69.16.2.

10 Spawforth (1999), 340.

11 Plutarch, *Life of Pericles* 17.1.

12 Plutarch, *Life of Pericles* 17.3; Thucydides, *Peloponnesian War* 1.23.6.

13 *IG* i³ 78 (= *IG* 1² 76).

14 Doukellis (2009), 294.

15 Spawforth (1999), 34.

16 Suetonius, *Vespasian* 23, 24.

17 *IG* VII 73, 74.

18 Dio Cassius 69.10.2; *CIL* XII 1122.

19 Thucydides, *Peloponnesian War* 2.41 (trans. Martin Hammond).

Chapter 10

1 *Epit. de Caes.* 14.8.

2 *HA Hadrian* 11.3.

3 *Epit. de Caes.* 14.9; *HA Hadrian* 23.9.

4 Eck (1978), 909–14.

5 From the Museo del Palazzo dei Conservatori in Rome, in Opper (2008), fig. 193.

6 Boatwright (2000), 523.

7 Opper (2008), 204.

8 Bernand (1960), nos 28–31.

9 Bowie (1990), 62.

10 *POxy.* VIII 1085, translation in Opper (2008), 172.

11 Opper (2008), 171.

12 Lambert (1984), 127.

13 Dio Cassius 69.11.2–3.

14 *HA Hadrian* 11.7.

15 Davidson (2007), 102.

16 Opper (2008), 168.

17 Williams (2010), 18.

18 *HA Hadrian* 11.7.

19 Williams (2010), 335, 263.

20 Williams (2010), 65.

21 Opper (2008), 169.

22 Athansius, *Apologia contra Arianos* 3.5.230.

23 Williams (2010), 64.

24 68.10.2.

25 *HA Hadrian* 14.9.

26 Opper (2008), 170.

27 Opper (2008), 173.

28 Statius, *Silvae* 2.1.

29 *HA Hadrian* 14.5.

30 Dio Cassius 69.11.3–4.

31 Moorhead and Stuttard (2012), 132.

32 Moorhead and Stuttard (2012), 132.

33 Moorhead and Stuttard (2012), 132.

34 Opper (2008), 188–90.

35 Opper (2008), 181.

Chapter 11

1 Cicero, *DND* 2.7.

2 Luke 23.4.22; Acts 25.8.

3 *Nero* 16.2.

4 *Annals* 15.44.

5 Pliny, *Letters* 10.96, 97.

6 Birley (1997), 125–7.

7 Eusebius, *HE* 4.3.

8 Goodman (2007), 440.

9 Josephus, *Bellum Judaicum* 6.241; Sulpicius Severus, *Chronica* 2.30.6–7.

10 *Parthica* in the *Suda* in Stern (1980), 152.

11 Birley (1997), 269; Dio Cassius 69.14.2.

12 Goodman (2007), 491.

13 24.17.

14 Opper (2008), 90.

15 69.12.2.

16 69.12.3.

17 Opper (2008), 95–7.

18 Tacitus, *Agricola* 30.

19 69.13.1.

20 Birley (1997), 268.

21 Birley (1997), 273. The advice would be *Poliorcetica*, attributed to Apollodorus.

22 Dio Cassius 69.14.3.

23 *HE* 4.6.2.

24 69.13.3–14.1.

25 69.14.3.

26 *HE* 4.6.3.

27 Rabbinic story: Schäfer (1981), 138.

28 Jerome, *In Esaiam* 1.2.9.

29 Jerome, *Chronica* 201 (Helm).

30 *CIL* XVI 87 of Nov. 139.

31 Pausanias 1.5.5.

Chapter 12

1   Victor, *Liber de Caesaribus* 14.1.4.

2   *HA Hadrian* 8.11.

3   Dio Cassius 69.16.3.

4   Birley (1997), 281.

5   *HA Hadrian* 23.4.

6   *HA Hadrian* 15.2.

7   *HA Hadrian* 15.4.

8   *HA Hadrian* 15.3.

9   Dio Cassius 69.18.4; *PIR²* M 249; Syme (1980).

10 Opper (2008), 215.

11 Opper (2008), 216.

12 Dio Cassius 69.17.1.

13 *HA Hadrian* 23.10, cf. *HA Aelius* 5.1.

14 *HA Aelius* 5.7, 5.11.

15 *HA Aelius* 5.9.

16 69.17.1.

17 *HA Hadrian* 23.15.

18 *HA Antoninus Pius* 4.5, 4.1.

19 *HA Hadrian* 23.11.

20 Dio Cassius 69.17.1; cf. *HA Hadrian* 15.8; 23.2, 8; 25.8.

21 Dio Cassius 69.17.2.

22 *HA Hadrian* 26.6.

23 Dio Cassius 69.20.1-3.

24 Birley (1997), 295-6.

25 Dio Cassius 69.20.1, 22.1.

26 69.22.1–4.

27 *HA Hadrian* 24.8–11.

28 Dio Cassius 69.11.2; *HA Hadrian* 7.2.

29 Papyrus of letter *PFayum* 19 in Smallwood (1966), 123 (trans. Birley).

30 Dio Cassius 66.17.1; Eutropius, *Breviarium* 7.21.

31 Dio Cassius 69.22.4.

32 *HA Hadrian* 25.6–7.

33 69.23.2 (he was hated by the people).

34 *HA Hadrian* 16.6; Birley (1997), 356n. 1. The Ennius echoes are from a fragment attributed to his *Andromache*.

35 *HA Hadrian* 14.11, cf. *Epit. de Caes.* 14.6.

36 Petrakis (1980), 87–91.

37 Birley (1997), 301.

38 *Orations* 26K 33.

Bibliography

Classical works

Aelius Aristides, *Orations*

Anthologia Palatina

Apuleius, *The Golden Ass (Metamorphoses)*

Aristotle, *History of Animals*

Arrian, *Parthica*

Athanasius, *Apologia contra Arianos*

Augustine, *Confessions*

Callistratus, *Digest*

Cato, *De Agricultura*

Cicero, *ad familiares*

—*De Natura Deorum*

—*Laelius*

CIL = *Corpus Inscriptionum Latinarum*

Clement of Alexandra, *Protrepticus*

Dio Cassius, *Roman History*

Ennius, *Andromache*

Epit. de Caes. = *Epitome de Caesaribus*

Eusebius, *Historia Ecclesiastica*

Eutropius, *Breviarium ab urbe condita*

Fronto, *Principia Historiae*

Galen

Gellius, *Noctes Atticae*

Greek Anthology

HA = *Historia Augusta: Hadrian, Aelius, Antoninus Pius, Verus*

Horace, *Satires*

IG = *Inscriptiones Graecae*

IGRom. = *Inscriptiones Graecae ad res Romanas pertinentes*

ILS = Dessau, *Inscriptiones Latinae Selectae*

Jerome, *Chronica*

Josephus, *Bellum Judaicum*
Juvenal, *Satires*
Mamertius, *Panegyric*
Martial, *De Spectaculis*
—*Epigrams*
Ovid, *Ars Amatoria*
—*Metamorphoses*
Pausanias
PFayum = *Fayum Papyri*
Philostratos, *Lives of the Sophists*
—*Vita Apollonii*
PIR = *Prosopographia Imperii Romani Saeculi I, II, III*
Pliny the Elder, *Natural History*
Pliny the Younger, *Letters*
—*Panegyricus*
Plutarch, *Caesar*
—*Pericles*
POxy = *Oxyrhynchus Papyri*
Propertius
RIC = Mattingly-Sydenham and others, *Roman Imperial Coinage*
SEG = *Supplementum Epigraphicum Graecum*
Seneca, *Letters*
Statius, *Silvae*
Strabo, *Geography*
Suda: a Greek lexicon
Suetonius, *Caligula*
—*Iulius* (Julius Caesar)
—*Nero*
—*Vespasian*
Sulpicius Severus, *Chronica*
Tacitus, *Agricola*
—*Annals*
Tertullian, *De spectaculis*
Thucydides, *History of the Peloponnesian War*
Victor, *Liber de Caesaribus*

Virgil, *Aeneid*
Xenophon, *On Hunting*

Other books and articles referred to in the text

J. P. V. D. Balsdon, *Life and Leisure in Ancient Rome* (1969, London: The
    Bodley Head)
M. Beard, *Pompeii, the Life of a Roman Town* (2008, London: Profile
    Books)
A. and E. Bernard, *Les inscriptions grecques et latines du Colosse de Memnon*
    (1960, Paris: Institut Français d'Archéologie Orientale)
A. R. Birley, *Hadrian, the Restless Emperor* (1997, Abingdon and New York:
    Routledge)
M. T. Boatwright, *Hadrian and the Cities of the Roman Empire* (2000,
    Princeton and Oxford: Princeton University Press)
—*Hadrian and the City of Rome* (1987, Princeton: Princeton University
    Press)
—'Hadrian' in A. A. Barrett (ed.), *Lives of the Caesars* (2008, Malden, MA:
    Blackwell), 155–80
E. Bowie, 'Greek Poetry in the Antonine Age' in D. Russell (ed.), *Antonine
    Literature* (1990, Oxford: Oxford University Press)
—'Greeks and their past in the Second Sophistic', *Past and Present* 46.1
    (February 1970), 3–41
D. J. Breeze, *The Frontiers of Imperial Rome* (2011, Barnsley: Pen and Sword
    Military)
B. Burrell, *Neokoroi, Greek Cities and Roman Emperors* (2004, Leiden and
    Boston, MA: Brill)
A. Claridge, 'Hadrian's Column of Trajan', *Journal of Roman Archaeology* 6
    (1993), 5–22
—*Rome* (1998, Oxford: Oxford University Press)
D. Danziger and N. Purcell, *Hadrian's Empire* (2005, London: Hodder and
    Stoughton)
J. Davidson, *The Greeks and Greek Love* (2007, London: Weidenfeld and
    Nicolson)

P. N. Doukellis, 'Hadrian's *Panhellenion*: A Network of Cities?' in I. Malkin,
   C. Constantakopoulou and K. Panagopoulou (eds), *Greek and Roman
   Networks in the Mediterranean* (2009, Abingdon: Routledge)

W. Eck, 'Vibia (?) Sabina, n. 72b', *RE Suppl.* 15 (1978)

A. Everitt, *Hadrian and the Triumph of Rome* (2009, London: Random
   House)

J. Fündling, *Kommentar zu Vita Hadriani der Historia Augusta 1* (2006,
   Bonn: Rudolf Habelt)

J. Godwin, 'Snails, Hairy Spiders, and Contraception', *Omnibus* 12 (1986)

M. Goodman, *Rome and Jerusalem, the Clash of Ancient Civilizations* (2007,
   London: Allen Lane)

R. Hannah and G. Magli, 'The Role of the Sun in the Pantheon's Design
   and Meaning', *Numen* 58 (2011), 486–513

M. Harlow and R. Laurence, *Growing Up and Growing Old in Ancient Rome*
   (2002, Abingdon: Routledge)

B. W. Henderson, *The Life and Principate of the Emperor Hadrian* (1923,
   London: Methuen)

S. J. Heyworth and J. H. W. Morwood, *A Commentary on Propertius,
   Book 3* (2011, Oxford)

K. Hopkins and M. Beard, *The Colosseum* (2005, London: Profile Books)

S. James, *Rome and the Sword* (2011, London: Thames and Hudson)

P. Jones and K. Sidwell (eds), *The World of Rome: an Introduction to Roman
   Culture* (1997, Cambridge: Cambridge University Press)

R. Lambert, *Beloved and God, the Story of Hadrian and Antinous* (1984,
   London: Phoenix)

R. Ling, 'Roman Art and Architecture' in Jones and Sidwell, 287–316

W. MacDonald and J. Pinto, *Hadrian's Villa and its Legacy* (1995, New
   Haven: Yale University Press)

F. Millar, *The Emperor in the Roman World* (1977, London: Duckworth)

S. Moorhead and D. Stuttard, *The Romans who Shaped Britain* (2012,
   London: Thames and Hudson)

T. Opper, *Hadrian* (2008, London: British Museum)

N. L. Petrakis, 'Diagonal Earlobe Creases, Type A Behavior, and the Death
   of Emperor Hadrian', *Western Journal of Medicine* 132 (January 1980),
   87–91

R. A. Pitcher, 'The Emperor and his Virtues: The Qualities of Domitian', *Antichthon* 24 (1990), 86–95

D. Rathbone, *Lives of Hadrian, Cassius Dio and the Historia Augusta* (2008, London: Pallas Athene)

J. S. Richardson, *The Romans in Spain* (1996, Oxford and Cambridge, MA: Blackwell)

R. T. Ridley, 'The Fate of an Architect: Apollodorus of Damascus', *Athenaeum* 77 (1989), 551–65

L. Rossi, *Trajan's Column and the Dacian Wars* (1971, London: Thames and Hudson)

J. Roth, *Roman Warfare* (2009, Cambridge: Cambridge University Press)

P. Schäfer, *Der Bar Kokhba-Aufstand* (1981, Bonn: Rudolf Habelt)

E. M. Smallwood, *Documents Illustrating the Principates of Nerva, Trajan and Hadrian* (1966, Cambridge: Cambridge University Press)

P. Southern, *The Roman Army, a Social and Institutional History* (2007, Oxford: Oxford University Press)

A. J. S. Spawforth, 'The Panhellenion Again', *Chiron* 29 (1999), 339–522

M. P. Speidel, *Emperor Hadrian's Speeches to the African Army – A New Text* (2006, Mainz: RGZM)

E. Speller, *Following Hadrian, A Second-Century Journey through the Roman Empire* (2002, Oxford, Oxford University Press)

D. Spencer, *Roman Landscape: Culture and Identity, Greece and Rome* (2010, Cambridge: Cambridge University Press)

M. Stern (ed.), *Greek and Latin Authors on Jews and Judaism, Volume 2* (1980, Jerusalem: The Israel Academy of Sciences and Humanities)

R. Syme, 'Guard Prefects of Trajan and Hadrian', *Journal of Roman Studies* 70 (1980), 64–80

J. Uden, *The Invisibility of Juvenal: Satire and Second-Century Rome* (forthcoming)

M. P. J. Van den Hout (ed.), *M. Cornelii Frontonis Epistulae* (1988, Leipzig)

C. Vout, *Power and Eroticism in the Roman World* (2007, Cambridge: Cambridge University Press)

C. Williams, *Roman Homosexuality* (2nd edn) (2010, Oxford: Oxford University Press)

M. Wilson Jones, *Principles of Roman Architecture* (2000, New Haven: Yale
   University Press)

M. Yourcenar, *Memoirs of Hadrian* (2000, London: Penguin)

P. Zsidi, 'Aquincum – the Capital of Pannonia Inferior. Topography of the
   Civil Town', in G. Hajnóczi, *La Pannonia e l'Impero Romano* (1994,
   Milan: Electa), 213–20

Index

Jerusalem 89, 90–1, 95
Jews 25, 89–95
Judaea 89–95
Julius Caesar 31
Juvenal 13–14, 47

lavatories 48
legions
    I Minervia 18
    II Adiutrix 15, 21
    V Macedonica 16
    VII Gemina 13
    XXII Primigenia 16
    Third Legion 92
    Tenth Legion 90, 95
    Twenty-Second Legion 92
Licinius Silvanus Granianus 88
Littlecote Villa 85
Lucius Ceionius Commodus,
        renamed Lucius Aelius Caesar
        101–2
Lucius Ceionius Commodus, son of
        the above 102

Mamertinus 57–8
Marcellus 98
Marcius Turbo 98
Marcus Annius Verus, the future
        emperor Marcus Aurelius 101,
        102–3
Martial 15, 52
Mastor 103
Matilda, Hadrian's mother-in-law 76
Mausoleum of Augustus 98–9, 100
Mausoleum of Hadrian 98–9
Mausoleum of Halicarnassus 100
Mesopotamia 25
Monte Testaccio 7

Nero, emperor 37, 88, 89
Nerva, emperor 16, 18, 90, 99

olive oil 6–8
Osiris 78, 83, 85

Ovid
    Amores 101
    Metamorphoses 12

P. Acilius Attianus 8
Palmyra 56
Panhellenia games 70
Panhellenion 2, 68–72
Pantheon 32–6, 42
Parthia 22, 23
Paulina, Hadrian's sister 84
Pausanias 95
Pedanius Fuscus 101–2
Pericles 69, 71–3
Pheidias 43, 66
Philostratos 41–2, 59, 60
Platorius Nepos 97–8
Pliny the Younger 53–4, 57, 88
Plotina, Trajan's wife 23, 56, 99
Polemon 59–60, 66–7, 85
Polyaenus 98
Pompey 51
Pons Aelius 99
Publicius Marcellus 92
Publius Claudius Pulcher 87
Puteoli 104

Q. Terentius Scaurus 8
Quintus Mucius Scaevola 10

Rabbi Akiba 91
religion 2, 70–1, 84–5, 87–96
    religious fundamentalism 87
Roman imperialism 93
Romanization 28, 29, 47–8
Rome 5, 7–8, 18–20, 31–7, 41, 48–9,
        51, 54, 66, 90, 95, 97, 98–101

Sabina, Hadrian's wife 2, 17, 29–30,
        72, 75–7, 78, 82, 102
St Augustine 50
Sappho 76
Scotland 93
Second Sophistic 8